The Gift of Tomorrow

JOURNEYS IN FAITH

The Gift of Tomorrow

Robert A. Raines

Journeys in Faith
Robert A. Raines, Editor

ABINGDON PRESS
Nashville

THE GIFT OF TOMORROW

Copyright © 1984 by Abingdon Press

Library of Congress Cataloging in Publication Data

RAINES, ROBERT ARNOLD.
 The gift of tomorrow.
 (Journeys in faith)
 1. Raines, Robert Arnold. 2. United Church of Christ—United
States—Clergy—Biography. I. Title. II. Series.

BX9886.Z8R358   1984   285.8'34'0924 [B]   83-25883

ISBN 0-687-14692-5

(credits continued on page 158)

MANUFACTURED BY THE PARTHENON PRESS AT
NASHVILLE, TENNESSEE, UNITED STATES OF AMERICA

To
Catharine, Barbara, Nancy, Sally,
Robert, Matthew,
and
all their sisters and brothers
in every country

Acknowledgments

Thanks to Abingdon Press for seeing the value in a Journeys in Faith book series and conspiring to make it happen with the necessary investment and commitment, and thanks to the editorial staff for competent and sensitive editing of all the books in the series, particularly my own.

Thanks to Irma Jarrett, diligent typist, and to Elizabeth and David Dodson Gray, Michael Clark, and Cynthia Hirni for careful criticism of portions of this book. Thanks to those who kindly allowed me to quote from portions of their letters.

Thanks to all who have helped convert me to the vocation of peacemaking.

Contents

Preface

This is the final book of the Journeys in Faith series. Series authors have been invited to share what has been happening to them in their faith and life in recent years, and then to focus on issues that have become primary for them in this time.

I have enjoyed and benefited from watching each author dig around his or her own faith roots towards the blossoming of these books. The continuity of particular denominational and ethnic heritage in the lives and work of my colleagues is notable. Thomas Merton has been frequently quoted in these books. Perhaps that is because solitude and community were not separated in him, but integrated in a spirituality that called him "to choose the world." The authors of these books struggle in different ways to heal or balance or bring together the inner and outer journeys. Bonhoeffer once said, "Let him who cannot be alone beware of community. Let him who cannot be in community beware of being alone." As Bonhoeffer seeded the post-World War II generation, perhaps Merton has seeded the post-Vietnam generation. In any case I resonate to Merton's longing to find and fulfill his vocation in a way that nourishes the soul while preserving the world.

This book comes out of the recent loss of my mother and father. Sweeping up the heart and hearth of their

lives and legacies has been turning me to work for the
preservation of the world for my own children and all
the little ones. The cloud of witnesses gone before
causes me to look over my shoulder at the cloud of
witnesses waiting, yearning to come after. Mourning
the death of my parents has opened me to mourn the
possible death of the planet, and to consider the fate of
the earth as the primary human and creaturely concern
of this era. I hope this book will contribute toward
keeping creation at ease.

Robert A. Raines
Glen Lake, Michigan

1
Sweeping Up the Heart

Kirkridge, Monday, September 21, 1981

The phone was ringing as the car drew up behind the house. I got out, ran up the steps, fumbled the lock open, and reached for the phone on the kitchen wall. My brother John was saying, "Bob, it's John. Bad news. Dad died this afternoon. Heart attack. Quickly."

Hammer blows. Dad died. Today. Monday, September 21, 1981. Dad is dead. My father is dead.

But he was so vigorous last summer, the first summer after mother died. Almost exactly a year ago now. Dad was striding through that summer up there at the family cottage in Michigan. One night he was having dinner with my family in the Big Cottage. When dinner was over he stood up from the table and took long, leaning steps toward the back door, falling over a chair unseen by his weak eyes. We helped him to his feet. Nothing serious, just a bruised knee. I shook my head. "Dad, you've got to be more careful!" But he wasn't being careful. He was striding right into the next chapter of his life and had been since before Easter.

Beloved Bob and Cindy,   Easter Morn, 1981

It is early on Easter morn, and I write with joy in my heart because in God's own good way and time I shall

13

be again with our beloved Lucille. This is the first Easter of my life when I have been without other dear ones around me. But God has provided dear friends here in Lakeland. . . . The trip to Indiana was a great joy. The preaching went well, and tired and worried me less than three months ago. Special luncheons and dinners gave intimate fellowship with ministers and wives. . . .

Then I was able to open the way for an appeal for five hundred thousand dollars more for the Franklin Methodist Home. . . . Then I had a beautiful time at the Lucille Raines Residence, put a lovely Easter lily under Lucille's picture, stayed for dinner, and shared my loss and faith with the friends after dinner—with remarkable responses, for they had all of them suffered. . . . Saw Dr. Nay who gave me a good report but cautioned about exercising too violently—exercise easily, and don't push things. . . . Got home OK Thursday night and am just now feeling rested and fit. I will go easier each day on my next trip, which begins this coming Saturday night—the council of bishops at Rapid City for Mother's memorial. . . .

Dad is dead. My father is dead.

John and I divided up the necessary telephoning. He had already talked with our sister Rose in Indianapolis. The family had gathered there a year ago for our mother's memorial service, and would gather there again in four days for my father's memorial service. I tried to reach my brother Dick in California, but no one answered.

There was Dad with open arms calling me to run to him. I was seven or eight years old, at Camp Lincoln near Alexandria, Minnesota. Dad and Mother had come to see me after I had been gone from home two weeks, my first separation from them. I was homesick. And there was Dad across the field in front of the camp headquarters, with his arms held out. I started to run and ran with all my might right into and up and around in those hugging arms swinging me around and around. My father loves me, this I know. And always I knew it, even when he was angry with me and I with him, even when things broke between us for a time, even when expressions of love were tight, terse. I always knew my father loved me and always would. Couldn't help himself.

All my childhood and perhaps much longer, I was running into his arms. I had a great protector who would always take care of me. He would come into my room late at night if I was sick or afraid, and rub my back, as his father had rubbed his back, as I would rub the backs of my children. Even when I had become a young man and was playing football for Yale against Wisconsin in the fall of 1948 at Madison, Dad came into the hotel where the Yale team was staying overnight before the game and rubbed my back. Yale won the game the next day, 17 to 7, and I had a very good day! I worshiped him, as he revered his own father, neither of us aware of the shadow in our fathers or ourselves. So the break between us in later years was the more astonishing and terrible.

I hear my father; I need never fear
I hear my mother; I shall never be lonely, or want for love.
When I am hungry it is they who provide for me; when I
am in dismay, it is they who fill me with comfort.
When I am astonished or bewildered, it is they who make

the weak ground firm beneath my soul: it is in them that I
put my trust.

When I am sick it is they who send for the doctor; when I
am well and happy, it is in their eyes that I know best that I
am loved; and it is towards the shining of their smiles that I
lift up my heart and in their laughter that I know my best
delight.

I hear my father and my mother and they are my giants, my
king and my queen, beside whom there are no others so wise
or worthy or honorable or brave or beautiful in this world.
I need never fear: nor ever shall I lack for lovingkindness.[1]

On Wednesday, September 23, I wrote in my journal:

The comfort I feel, the gathering of the family; we'll
all be there again in Rose's home, the pilgrimage with
John to the graveside in Independence [Iowa], where
I will grieve and mourn. Dad and Mother now. "Lord
heal and forgive all in me, between Dad and me and
me and Dad; thank You for the fierce persistence of
his love, and his righteousness, which he obeyed for
himself . . . and his patriarchy of our family, which
has given us some sense of special destiny, belonging,
and vocation."

And on Thursday, September 24: I want to
experience my father's death, to go with him all the
way to Independence, to go home with him. I want to
be present in love and trust with John, Dick, Rose and
all the family . . . our patriarch is gone . . . the mighty
oak fallen. I want to be comforted and drawn
together with my children. . . . I want to know the
meaning of my father's life and to be further freed to
love him and receive his love.

Indianapolis, Friday, September 25

Rose and Bob (her husband) . . . for twenty years they did the support work for Mother and Dad in the period of Dad's Indiana episcopacy. Taking them to planes, meeting other planes, but never once flying away from that airport themselves. Taking care of the folks' house when they were away, which was often and for long periods. Taking care of them when sick or lonely. Participating in numerous celebrations honoring them. Mother and Dad were, in a modest manner for a time, the King and Queen of the Methodists in Indiana. Rose stood often in courtly waiting, with Bob there too. On one such occasion, all the children were flown in secretly for a "This Is Your Life" celebration. We children were the piéce de résistance. A whooping, hilarious night of singing the old hymns and telling stories on the folks. That audience of Methodist lay people and clergy heard my word about their bishop with roaring delight: "My father reminds me of Jesus . . . who said, 'You are my friends, if you do what I command you.' "

My sister Rose . . . from whom I felt remote for how many years . . . since we were children? My sister whom I didn't need, whom I scarcely saw all those years when we were together at family anniversaries, celebrations, gatherings at Glen Lake. It was my brothers and I who were doing the "valuable, interesting, important" things in our ministries. All three of us sons went into the ministry.

My sister Rose, whose comfort I had needed since the time of my divorce in 1974, whose sisterhood I wanted. I began to stop off and visit Rose and Bob overnight in Indianapolis whenever I was preaching or speaking out their way. Slowly, guardedly, we reached out to touch each other. The distrust of the dust-laden years of neglect. The hurt of not being regarded. The carefulness of honest feeling disentangled from sentimentality.

One time, on my way in from the Indianapolis airport to see them, I stopped at a roadside florist to pick up a gift for her. The man took me around to the side of his stand and showed me some flowers. I heard him saying, "Here's a lovely Peace rose." I looked. Yellow! Beautiful! I bought it and took it to her. On my next visit she showed me how it was flourishing in their front yard.

On one of those visits we hugged each other goodbye and I said to her, "I love you." She leaned back, looked up into my eyes, and said, "Bob, I think you really do."

Rose and Bob—Bob about whom my father once said, "I sometimes feel closer to him than to my own sons." He is a physician, was my parents' family doctor. He could always reassure them, steady them when either of them feared some sickness or disability. He was always there. They could count on him. Stubborn, opinionated, gentle with those he could love and understand—a brother-in-law who has long been a brother-in-deed to me and my brothers.

It was good to be in their familiar living room again. A year ago, when we were all there, Dad was rocking back and forth in the antique wooden rocker beside the fireplace, telling stories about Mother and about their courting days along the Wapsipinicon River, which flowed through Independence, Iowa, where they grew up. All at once he cried out, and said, "I need your consolation." I don't remember ever seeing my father cry before that moment.

Now there was comfort in the sheer numbers of us, the oldest touching sixty and the youngest yet in the womb. We swapped stories, sang some of the gospel songs we had learned in our childhood—"Precious Jewels," "I Am So Glad," "Sweet By and By," "He Leadeth Me," and "When the Mists Have Rolled Away." The latter song the four Raines men had often sung together, Dad taking either the bass or tenor, having the best voice of us all, save perhaps Dick. We sang it now with Rose taking Dad's place.

> When the mists have rolled in splendor
> From the river and the rills
> And the sunlight falls in gladness
> O'er the beauty of the hills
> We recall our Father's promise
> On that bright and happy day,
> We shall know each other better
> When the mists have rolled away.
> We shall know as we are known,
> Never more to walk alone.

Laughing at the proud and gleeful harmony, the sonorous tones, the rolling memories, looking at one another's faces and nodding, hands grasped around the room, generations united in a deeper bond than the ordinary words and common tune could convey.

I sat, alone, in the back of the room at the funeral home. The massive, cold, columned funeral establishment. Kind and courteous helpers there. My father's casket sat against the far wall. He had told me once that he had been comforted by seeing and touching his father's hands folded on his chest as he lay in his casket. Earlier I had noticed my father's hands lying at the side of his body . . . those gnarled hands . . . that played doggedly on the old piano in the basement of the Big Cottage at Glen Lake. Dad would play after dinner down there. It might be a lilting tune like "The Storybook Ball" or most often—a hymn. The sounds came through the floor of the cottage and couldn't be ignored by those upstairs. Sometimes I felt intruded upon or that playing was his way of getting our attention. I could see him looking out of his heavy glasses down onto the keyboard, fingers stumbling over the keys, the shining spirit of his face. But now, I saw his body in the casket fifty feet away against the other wall:

> His profile wakens the pillow
> Sculpting a mountain there;
> The nose flares up, then gravely descends;
> A stallion strides down the ravine.[2]

That nose! That is my father. My father's nose: large, prominent, obdurate—image of his authority, integrity, righteousness—he who knew so little of his own dark side. That nose. Dad was often stroking his nose—while talking, arguing, preaching, laughing. There he was in the old family movies, stroking his nose. We boys learned to stroke our noses too, but he was *the* nose-stroker. My giant, towards the shining of whose smile I lived my life under blue skies for over forty years.

My father is dead.

The memorial service took place at Roberts Park

United Methodist Church, Indianapolis, the church where my father had been ordained a bishop in 1948. Jim Armstrong and Ed Garrison, colleagues of Dad, took part with grace and affection. Our families gathered pew by pew. Afterwards, the friends—familiar and unfamiliar faces. And the words from dozens of people: "Your father married us thirty years ago." "Your father ordained me into the ministry." "Your father baptized all four of our children." I never knew a man like your father." Nor did I.

Independence, Iowa, Sunday, September 27

John and I had decided that we would carry our father's ashes to Independence, Iowa, for burial in the Raines family graveyard there. Dad was born and grew up in Independence, Mother in Oelwein, not far distant. A year before, Dick had accompanied Dad as he carried Mother's ashes to that burial place. Now it was our turn.

We had been invited to stay with Oliver and Lea Greenley of Independence, old friends of our parents, with whom Dad and Dick stayed the year before. They asked if they could meet us at the Cedar Rapids airport and take us into their home during our brief stay. The Greenleys are members of the First United Methodist Church in Independence, where my paternal grandparents and my father had been members. They showed us a book celebrating the one hundred twenty-fifth anniversary of that church. Pictures, a bit of history, and several items from the minutes of church meetings—one of which read:

1909—R. B. Raines was appointed a committee of one to ask the ladies to remove their
hats during morning and evening service.

Times had changed since the day of Paul, and my
grandfather, for whom I was named, was evidently a
fearless and courtly negotiator.

*Robert Bielby Raines. I remember him in family movies,
looking imperiously at Dad, smiling, stroking his nose, both of
them arguing vociferously about something. He was the lay
leader of the church during most of Dad's youth. He sang bass
in the church quartet for forty years and led the congregation in
hymn singing every Sunday night before the evening service
began.*

My father remembered: "He knew all the hymns by
heart. One Sunday evening an 'unbeliever' came to
evening service. He like to sing. He said to a friend, 'I'm
going to be here every Sunday night until that damn
song leader doesn't know a hymn by heart!' The
unbeliever came until at the end of some weeks, he was
converted and joined the church."

My father adored his father, who had worked himself
up to become president of the Farmer's State Savings
Bank in Independence, lost it all in the great crash of
1929, and needed, proud man that he was, help in his
later years. My father and mother sent both their
parents monthly checks over many years up until the
time of their deaths.

Dad was twelve years old when his eighteen-year-old
brother Jean died of appendicitis. The doctor operated
on Jean on the family dining room table; there was
infection, peritonitis set in, and Jean died. Grandpa was
wild with grief, Dad said. He carried Jean's lifeless body

around the house for hours that night. It broke
something in him. And after that, when neighbors or
friends were struck with a death in the family, Grandpa
would go to see them and sit with them, for he had
walked that sorrowing valley himself. He and Grandma
often took my father with them, that little boy of twelve,
who thus saw a good deal of death and grieving—and
more, witnessed his parents' faith and compassion. The
deep pastoral soul of my father's vocation was perhaps
born, and surely nourished, in those neighborly visits.

My father learned a great many hymns by heart
himself, and my siblings and I learned to love singing
the old hymns, too. We sang hymns and songs as a
family, in morning devotions, riding in the car on
family vacations, or gathered around the fireside at
night in the summer. We had to go to church in the
summertime on vacation. Other kids didn't, we noted,
but we did. It seemed we often arrived a bit late, and
had to be ushered—often seven of us, including Helen
Latta, our family helper—up to one of the first pews.
We were embarrassed, but I think Dad was proud that,
once again, he had corralled his whole family to attend
worship. He liked peppermints in those days, the kind
that were white, circular, about one-eighth of an inch
thick. Two or three times during the service, usually
before the long pastoral prayer and the sermon, he
passed peppermints down the line to each of us. He
called it our "punishment." "Ready for punishment?"
he would whisper; we nodded, grinned. Surrepti-
tiously, they would come down the line, to be grasped
and taken to the mouth in a fashion as though one were
scratching one's chin or stroking one's nose—so no one
else would notice. It was fun. And it makes me smile to

remember how Dad sweetened the pious duties he imposed on us.

I can see Dad at Hennepin Avenue Church, or in one of those small summer churches, rocking back on his heels, belting out the chorus of "All Hail the Power of Jesus' Name." I became something of a belter, too, and to this day my heart is vulnerable to the Spirit in between the words and melodies of some of the great hymns, and some of the not-so-great as well. I know there's a strain of sentimentality in me, but I also know that when I sing with all my heart, there is a letting go of control and a rush of rolling joy. Dad would sing "O For a Thousand Tongues" as though one tongue were simply not enough to do it properly. It wasn't excessively loud; it was simply wholehearted.

In the last few years, Dad began to write hymn melodies. He got the organist at his Florida church to score them for him, and he would play them on the piano at home and up at Glen Lake. He asked me to compose words for one of these melodies. I did, and published the hymn, which is printed below.

I am glad that we collaborated on this hymn together, though I have few chances to sing it or hear it sung by a congregation. It is appropriate that the words derive from Psalm 121, one of his and my favorite psalms, and a song that we children were required to learn one summer vacation. That summer, for whatever reason, Dad was determined that his children would learn several psalms by heart. The bargain was clear: learn a psalm in the morning—get a bottle of soda pop in the afternoon. No psalm, no pop. It was a hot summer. We learned many psalms. Terrible pedagogy, but effective memorization. Over my objections, the liturgy crept

GOD WILL KEEP YOUR LIFE

Text based on Psalm 121
Words by
ROBERT A. RAINES
July 12, 1926

Music by
BISHOP RICHARD C. RAINES
December 23, 1898

Not Too Slowly
VERSE

1. I will lift my eyes to Thee, Au - thor of my birth.
2. He will lead you on the way Hold - ing in his hand,
3. He'll pro - tect you from all fears, Of the day or night

My help comes from Thee, oh Lord, Who made heav'n and earth.
Ev - er watch - ing, sleep - ing not, Strength - 'ning you to stand.
Shel - ter - ing and shad - ing you In His heal - ing light.

REFRAIN

God will keep you from all ill In sor - row, pain or strife,

Go - ing out and com - ing in, God will keep your life.

into my bones in those months, and I am glad that I know whole psalms and verses of others by heart now, in the King James Version, of course.

At 11:00 a.m. on Monday, September 28, the Greenleys stood with me and John, the United Methodist minister, and a few neighbors and friends by the graveside in the Oakwood Cemetery. The Raines family plot is towards the end of the graveyard road. The tombstones are to the left, a few inches above the earth, with the names of those buried engraved on the stone: Robert Bielby (Grandpa), Cora (Grandma), Rose (Dad's baby sister who died of pneumonia at the age of one and for whom my sister Rose is named), Jean, Ruth (Dad's retarded sister), Lucille (my mother), and then the open ground for the urn bearing my father's ashes. The Greenleys asked if they might give our family the urn, as they had done the year before for my mother's ashes. The kindly and generous ways of friendship.

I was comforted that there was a particular place where my parents' ashes lay, a particular piece of ground, this earth right here. I knew, as I stood there, that this was the end of the line for the Raines family in Independence, Iowa. None of our parents' four children would be buried there. Something was ending here, while continuing elsewhere. I was satisfied. I was glad I made the Iowa pilgrimage with John and saw my father and mother home.

Lakeland, Florida, Wednesday, October 14, 1981

Two weeks later, Rose, Dick, John, and I journeyed to our parents' retirement home in Florida. We had decided to spend three days together cleaning up, going through files and furniture, and gathering up the

loose ends of our parents' lives. Tom Watson, our
parents' attorney, helped us settle the estate. Furniture
appraisers, bank people, movers, friends, and neighbors came and went.

Dad must have kept every sermon he ever wrote on
file. He used to send me sermons now and then when I
was in the Navy. Here was a letter to him from me
saying how "delighted" I was to receive those sermons—keep them coming. A dutiful son! Pictures,
albums, tapes—what to save, what to throw away, who
to take what, what finally to put in a modest family
archive in Dad's study up at Glen Lake. The folks had
been specific about assignment of particular pieces of
furniture, paintings, china, objects, even to several
items for each grandchild and the two great grandchildren. We were glad that most of it had been decided for
us.

We cleaned, reminisced, talked, laughed, cried
together, and began to look at each other with fresh
eyes—the eyes of orphans. No longer did we have an
overhead shelter. Our heads were naked. And because
we could not look up any longer, we began to look
around—and saw each other. The last night there, we
went out "on the estate" for a marvelous dinner. Dick
wrote about it later to my wife Cindy:

Cindy, I wish you could have been with us! Probably
you've had enough "Raines trips"—but over all, this
get-together was genuinely healing—lots of honest
talk. It became clear to me that all four children truly
suffered and truly profited from the parents'
existence—a *good* experience filled with all the
pathos, depth of love, humor and anger that a real

wake would embrace . . . around it all was a union and bonding and a celebration and a frank enjoyment of the many lovely things the folks bequeathed to us all . . . a *great* way to do it and a great time to do it for us all. I wouldn't have had it any other way.

Nor I, nor any of us, I think.

During those days I kept remembering a "sweeping" image from an Emily Dickinson poem. I mentioned it finally to Cindy, and she located the poem.

> The Bustle in a House
> The Morning after Death
> Is solemnest of industries
> Enacted upon Earth—
>
> The Sweeping up the Heart,
> And putting Love away
> We shall not want to use again
> Until Eternity.[5]

Yes that was it. We were sweeping up the heart and hearth of our parents' lives and stirring up the soil of our own. And like the woman in that parable of Jesus, we were to be surprised again and again by lost coins of beauty and pain as we swept and wept and crept through the dark corridors of memory.

The year before, while I was visiting Dad in Lakeland, he had taken me with him one evening to his church. He was doing a Bible study on the Book of James. As I sat there, I remembered an early such journey we had made together when I was a child, perhaps eight or ten. We drove from Minneapolis in the yellow convertible car of a friend, Algot Johnson, to some church near Minneapolis where Dad was preaching. I suppose the seed of my own pastoral and preaching vocation was planted and nourished on such journeys with my father. Too many times to count in later years, people would come up to me after they heard me preach or speak, to tell me, not that they valued what *I* had said that night, but that they would "never forget" hearing my father at Cleveland in 1948, or in Baltimore, or wherever.

Most of the time I enjoyed that immensely, and was astonished at how many people could remember a sermon title or phrase such as "He Went a Little Farther," "Use it or Lose it," "Come Ye Apart." One of Dad's friends remembered an occasion when he had preached on that latter text, ending with the prayer, "O Lord, we have come apart before Thee this day . . ."!

Dad was one great preacher! And as with all preachers, it was better done in church than at home. I still remember a moment on a Florida beach years before, when he had rendered his judgment on my decision toward divorce.[4] It was the most painful moment in our relationship, healed now, but the sorrow not entirely gone. I hope we shall know each other better when the mists have rolled away.

Kirkridge, Late Fall, 1982

Death releases a trap door. We are falling down, down, down . . . to God. An orphan can't return to parents for nurture, but can fall down into the lap of God. Leaning on those everlasting arms in those months, I was comforted with the spiritual gifts of friends—the most astonishing insights and under-

standing. One wrote, "You are in our prayers as you
return to Kirkridge and take up your life once more. It
will have a new quality because some qualities will have
entered your spirit from your father's spirit as his
parting 'blessing' to you."

What a lovely idea! A parting blessing. I began to be
aware of many parting blessings.

One was a fresh freedom to acknowledge, with a kind
of unalloyed gratitude, some of the ways in which I am
like my father. One time Dad sent to Cindy and me a
letter from Indiana friends of his. They were participants in a midlife journey retreat Cindy and I
conducted for some members of the Indiana Conference of the United Methodist Church. Dad wrote,
"Maybe you won't like this, but they write, 'Gloria and
Joe were there with us too, and Gloria was almost
overwhelmed that Bob seemed to have many of your
mannerisms and facial expressions while speaking.
Guess I felt your presence there with Bob.' " Probably
some nose-stroking going on. Well, I *did* like that
observation, and find that I *am* glad to be like my father
in some ways, though I remember him as more
charismatic and filled with *joie de vivre* than I am.

I feel my connection with my father perhaps more
deeply than to any other human being, as though a
spiritual umbilical cord had not quite been severed, or
rather, that it is even now being reknit. Despite the
intimate distance, the chasm of silence . . . "Dad, your
arms and hands are around me, on me, and I am
fiercely proud to be your son."

I think all of us children, though sometimes angry at
him, were filled with a certain awe of him, too. One of
his favorite Bible verses was from the Twenty-third

Psalm: "Goodness and mercy shall follow me all the days of my life." He believed that goodness and mercy *had* followed him all the days of his life, that God's grace had blessed him and his family. As I have been responding to letters and cards and discovering letters in Dad's files, it is abundantly clear that much goodness and mercy followed in the wake of my father's ministry.

I received a letter from a friend dated March 3, 1983:

> Bob in going through some old correspondence not long ago, I found the enclosed letter. I was raised an Indiana Methodist, and my father was an active lay leader. He disdained to serve under the previous bishop whom he cordially despised, and I acquired an aversion to Methodism in the process. So I wrote to our new bishop within a few weeks after my decision to switch from biophysics to the ministry. And this is the letter I got. It meant a lot to me, as you can imagine, and it opened the door to consider Methodism again. . . . Although I eventually became a Presbyterian, I always regarded your father as a kind of mentor.

The letter from my father reads in part:

> Dear Edgar, [August 25, 1949]
> It is good to know that with your scientific training you are now definitely turning to the ministry. . . . I do not believe that it is very important which denomination suits you best. I believe that the most important next decision . . . is what school of theology you will attend. Since you have been reared and gone to school in the Middle West, there would

be a number of advantages in your taking your graduate theological work in the East. The Unitarian Church is certainly doing some fine social work; so also are the Quakers; so also are the Methodists and the Congregationalists. The problems which you mention will not settle themselves all at once, but if you keep working along day by day, reading, thinking, praying, giving your life into God's hands, seeking his will, disciplining yourself in the doing of it—one by one the problems will be solved, and you will be fruitfully used and will find the peace and happiness that come therefrom. May you have great joy as you prepare for and enter into the ministry. (The signature, Richard C. Raines, is as strong and clear as though Dad had written it yesterday.)

It is hard to improve on that counsel of thirty-five years ago.

I know that goodness and mercy have followed and preceded me throughout my life because of him, doors have been opened, exceptions made, preferences extended. I trust that my father understands, knows, how proud and glad I am to be even a little like him, even as I retain some sorrow that my full gratitude waited upon his death for its realization. We are, of course, different too, as different as our generations, worlds, souls, life histories.

Another friend, whose father yet lives, wrote,

The death of your father is a life-changing moment . . . one of loss and sorrow and also a kind of freedom and drawing of your father's qualities into yourself. I know for myself that my father is such a powerful figure in my life that I am often aware of powerful currents of feeling: both a wish that he die and stop impeding progress and an enormous love and compassion and respect for who he is and what he has achieved. Mostly, I hope he'll live forever. Your father's death reactivates these thoughts. . . . good blessings to you in this new phase of your life where you are now the "father" of your family.

I *do* feel ambivalence about my father's death. Both grief and relief. He was the most powerful shaping presence in my life. In some sense I lived a long time trying to please him, for some part of that time not understanding that I was also trying to please my father-God. He was the model for my manhood and my ministry, the earthly image of my heavenly father.

So pervasive was our paternal shaping that my two brothers and I all went to seminary and into some form of ministry. As for me, it wasn't until my middle age, and with wrenching pain, that I made choices taking me in different directions from those my father would have chosen—clearing and fencing off my own life-space, separate from his. My own heart was torn for him as he struggled to understand in these recent years why it was and how it was that his children needed some "space" from him. His relationship with his parents, and especially his father, had been so intimate. His parents actually accompanied him and my mother on part of their honeymoon, tenting on opposite sides of the car in Yellowstone. And when relatives visited his parents in the summertime, his parents moved out of their bedroom, tenting on the lawn so that the relatives could be properly made welcome in the house. No wonder

Dad thought families should all be close like that.

In the years while I was dis-assembling and then re-assembling my life, the time at Glen Lake was tension-filled. Three cottages there: the Big Cottage where I and my blended family lived; the Upper Room, one hundred feet up the hillside in the woods; and the folks' place, the Last Resort, on the same level as the Big Cottage, about ten yards to the north. The spacious porch of the Big Cottage faces east, looking out over the lake. It is screened, with one section on both south and north sides. There are latticed shades for all screened sections, to be used in a rainstorm.

Through the years the shades on *all* screens were usually up, including the one on the north side facing the folks' cottage. Thus, anybody on our porch could be seen from the folks' windows and vice versa. Every morning there would be nods, called out "hellos," "when are you going to town?" and so on. The time came when those innocent morning greetings became intolerable intrusions, when one began to feel moni- tored, observed, evaluated, hemmed in, crowded. (Who goes on vacation for a month with his parents ten yards away the whole time? I did! For over thirty years.)

One morning I put the north shade down. It stayed down as long as my parents lived. They were hurt by the shade being down, although Mother could understand it better than Dad. He wanted and needed to be with people much of the time, but after awhile she would retire, go back to their cottage—withdraw in some way. Dad played countless games of backgammon and rummy with his grandchildren and his step-grandchildren, and they loved it. They didn't understand the tensions between me and my parents and didn't want to hear about it or my need for space. I suspect they will understand more as they deal with their own need for space from me in years to come! I realize more clearly now my own enveloping, pervasive parenting of my children. I know that I need to restrain and contain myself in order to allow them more freely to shape their own lives. If I want them to take initiative in communicating with me, I must sometimes suffer the pain of waiting.

Henri Nouwen writes about the "art of leaving," and suggests that we all need to cultivate the ability to be articulately absent—the capacity for creative withdrawal.[5] We need to grow into a maturing interplay between absence and presence in developing a style of parenting, spousing, befriending, which encourages the autonomy of the other.

The art of leaving. God's way. In one of his last conversations with his friends, Jesus said, "It is to your advantage that I go away, for if I do not go away, the Counselor will not come to you" (John 16:7). By a creative withdrawal of himself, Jesus allowed the Spirit to abide in us always and everywhere as comforter, guide, companion. God trusts us enough to leave us alone in this world, in the Spirit.

So my father's death, after the death of my mother, has allowed the Spirit to come into my ken, my heart, my life—from darker depths with brighter light. Grieving is a dismemberment that opens the way for a re-membering. In those months of re-membering, I rediscovered the communion of the saints.

A friend wrote:

All relationships are unique and each break with the flow of patterns in this life has a peculiar combination of loss and gain. The loss of my father still affects me more than any other. At the same time, I am almost closer to him and sense his presence more than when he was alive but geographically distant. Spiritual space is marvelously intimate space and has an incredible spontaneity about it. I did not know your father, but the very fact that you followed his vision in Christian witness, adding your own special touch and insights gives some clue to your closeness. Cherish your memories!

I am cherishing my memories, and often am taken by surprise. Some nights at dusk, sipping a drink and leaning back in the folks' old rocker, I remember with a flow of smiles how Dad got rid of the Queen of Spades and won yet another game of Hearts—or that time in our Minneapolis childhood, when Dick and I had not shoveled the sidewalks after a snowstorm, and Dad with his sinus trouble went outside and shoveled the walks and wouldn't let us help him, and it was Saturday and he could become ill on Sunday . . . he knew how to make us feel guilty! And often we were. I am groping now like a stranger in that country of spiritual space . . . faces appear . . . and hands . . . and that nose . . . and one strains to remember the sound of the familiar voice. It does comfort me that my "following his vision" is an abiding clue to our closeness.

One morning, a few months after Mother's death, a letter from Dad arrived addressed to me. In it he said simply, "I woke up this morning, to find the barrier between us gone. I didn't do anything. It was gone when

I woke up. I know you have had no barrier to me since Mother's death. Now, thank God, mine is gone too."

I am becoming more content to acknowledge the mystery of our love for one another, the woundedness of fathers and sons, and to rest with him in the communion of saints. That communion is more palpable to me now, especially in the sharing of bread and wine. "Do this in remembrance of me." Sometimes in the eucharist I feel the cloud of witnesses surrounding me and all of us, our angels of forgiveness and healing, our balcony people, our cheering section. The communion of the saints. Oh, the wisdom of the church! Those eight words in the Apostles' Creed waiting all those centuries and all the years of my life, until I could begin to understand my yearning for their truth even a little. Like a chord of a great symphony one didn't notice for the beauty and magnificence of other chords, until one day, or rather one night, that quiet chord of truth sounds with a sweet, clear depth—deep calls to deep—a sound that cannot be heard in the ear until it has broken in the heart.

I believe in the communion of the saints, though I do not know much of what it means. Frederick Buechner writes: "On All Saints' Day, it is not just the saints of the church that we should remember in our prayers, but all the foolish ones and wise ones, the shy ones and overbearing ones, the broken ones and whole ones, the despots and tosspots and crackpots of our lives who, one way or another, have been our particular fathers and mothers and saints, and whom we loved without knowing we loved them and by whom we were helped to whatever little we may have, or ever hope to have, of some kind of seedy sainthood of our own."[6]

The society of seedy saints. There's room for many of us in such a society, perhaps in grace, all the poor human family, with our crazy failures, glorious successes, blessed messes, tragic mistakes, pathetic foolishness. My paternal grandmother once said to my father, "Richard, if I find once I get to heaven that all these years I could just as well have danced and played cards, I shall be very angry." My frail, gentle, wistful grandmother . . . angry? I would like to see it. She has a right, and God will applaud while the angels laugh.

Glen Lake, July 1982

Many of us have homing places, where the veil between heaven and earth is sometimes thin. Glen Lake is one of these for me. "The ties of this place are attached to very important points within my soul,"[7] and not mine alone. One discovery my brothers and I made in the context of our sweeping, was that each of us, independently and unknown to the others, had decided to deposit his ashes somewhere up at the lake, on the cottage grounds, or in a nearby cemetery. Tongue in cheek, I warn my children that my favorite spot for ash scattering may be the lake shore right at the dock, so that as they go swimming every day, I will be haunting them forever! Grim—but I am reluctant, even in imagination, to let them go. How dare they live full and fruitful lives without me around! In any case, I found myself satisfied and content that my parents' ashes were located in small urns and buried in a particular piece of ground. So I may suggest to my sweepers that my ashes be located, not scattered. Could I be trying to avoid physical dissolution and holding out for some tiny pile

of me, or is there something finally peaceful about the
ground of a particular place?

Glen Lake provides a unique continuing context for
my sweeping. We own a bit of land on the west hillside
of that lake. Thirty-four years ago my parents bought
this land and the Big Cottage for $3,000, a bargain even
then, though it was referred to by locals, not without
reason, as "the pea green shack on the damn hill." It was
the summer of 1949. My father and mother were
exhausted by their first year in Indiana, where Dad was
bishop of the Indiana area of the Methodist Church.
Friends told them of a lovely lake in Michigan and an
inn named Tonawathya on the west side of the lake.
They spent two weeks there—healing, restoring, taking
rides through the woods and down the back roads,
discovering hidden views of Glen Lake and of Lake
Michigan, only a mile away, and all the time falling in
love with the place. Tonawathya was comprised of a
rambling main building, yellow frame, a long porch
with wicker rockers, a staid, quiet dining room with
wicker chairs, and tables with fresh flowers and linens.
Several out-buildings, little cottages, and a barn
completed the scene, one of the cottages being at the
upper edge of the property—namely, the pea green
shack! It had, in fact, been built originally for a minister,
and in the stone steps leading up to the porch, were
engraved the words "Glen Glorious." Dad persuaded
Asa Case, the owner, who wanted to sell Tonawathya,
that he could get just as much for it with or without that
rundown cottage. And Dad was probably right. And
perhaps—Asa Case liked Mother and Dad. In any case,
the deal was made, the money was borrowed, and my
homing place became flesh in prospect.

In the early years of its use, my parents and, successively, my family and the families of my siblings, all lived together in the Big Cottage. Our vacations ranged from two weeks to a month, so it was a long time living together, using the same kitchen, the one bathroom. (Somewhat like the scene when relatives came to visit my Iowa grandparents decades ago.) But, as children were born and we became more numerous and vociferous, the folks retreated up the hill twenty-five yards and built the Upper Room. Then, years after that, as it became troublesome to climb up the hill to that dwelling, and as grandchildren wanted to sleep up there away from *their* parents, the folks built the Last Resort.

I knew all through the winter and spring of 1982 that something remained yet to be done and to be experienced—being at Glen Lake with both Mother and Dad gone. On Tuesday, June 29, 1982, we drove along the west side of the lake to the gravel road running up the hill to our cottages. When we came to turn off Route M-22 and started up the hill road, we honked the horn, saluting in memory the annual practice that had brought the waiting folks running out to the steps. Greeting us with open arms, they usually offered a plate of brownies, a can of peanuts, bottles of olives, or other goodies in the kitchen . . . all the little treats, along with flowers in vases in many rooms, which shouted "Welcome!"

But this time we drove up to a silent, dark cottage, and noticed immediately that there were no petunias in the window boxes. How drab the porch façade looked without those purple, red, white petunias!

My heart sank at the sight of the broken-down back

stoop, all the green shades down for the winter, the weedy plot in front of the porch where Dad grew his valiant roses, the patch by the folks' cottage where Mother's pansies always were. Where were the keys to the Upper Room? We forgot to arrange for the phone to be reconnected. The dock isn't in. . . .

So, the sweeping began that summer of 1982.

Brother Dick arrived soon after we got there that summer. While cleaning out the Last Resort, we found the family movies hidden away in a closet. One night we showed a few of our favorite reels. All of us, especially the children, have our own favorites, which show us in ridiculous or heroic action. One of the most popular film clips shows Bob Jr. at age four or five, when he was just learning to row the rowboat. We see him out in the boat about fifty yards from the dock. He is struggling with the oar, now lifting the oars up, taking a mighty stroke, which turns out to be a great whiff in the air, Bob disappearing below the gunwales of the boat, having missed the water entirely, and a few seconds later, rising to his feet with raging fists over his public failure. Movies of picnics on the beach—the first successful swimming efforts of each child and grandchild—anniversaries—birthdays. Even a couple of baptisms are recorded, along with every summer's numerous visitors. It was at Glen Lake that the children's friends, lovers, spouses, hangers-on, were looked over and looked us over. Any who survived the Glen Lake gantlet were numbered among the blessed, even if only (as it often turned out) of blessed memory.

Our own friends visited too. One afternoon in the summer of 1969, my father, Jim Armstrong, Bill Coffin, and I sat on the deck of the Last Resort. Bill was visiting his daughter Amy at the Interlochen Music Camp a few miles away, and Jim was the summer preacher at the Leland Community Church twelve miles north of us. The coincidence of their visit contained the delicious irony that all three of us—Jim, Bill and I—had been rejected the year before as candidates for the position of senior minister at the Riverside Church in New York City. Ernie Campbell got the job that time, though Bill was to make it to that particular throne of grace some years later, and Jim eventually returned to Indiana as the bishop of the United Methodist Church there. I smile to remember it.

I remember the early years as joyous family times of play, fun, swimming, games of Hearts, singing in harmony, canoeing, sailing, and water skiing, and then watching the children do it all. Learning as I had from my father, I spent the morning hours on vacation studying up at the Upper Room, reading, preparing sermon series for the coming year, writing. I wrote the first draft of most of my books up at the lake, just as I wrote the first chapter of this book there in the summer of 1982. I had decided to start writing this book at Glen Lake. The timing was right in terms of the publishers' deadline, long since gone beyond. But more importantly, I *wanted* to start writing it there—in my father's study, sitting at my father's desk. And, would you believe, wearing my father's shoes! You see, brother John got Dad's academic robes because he teaches at a university and presumably would have occasion to don them. But I got the shoes because both Dick's and John's feet are too big for Dad's shoes! My brothers, I love ya' cause your feets too big! (Fats Waller, eat your heart out!) So I got three pairs of shoes, two of them

Wallabys—soft, supple leather. Marvelous shoes. They just slide onto my feet like slippers. Talk about "walking in my father's footsteps!"

Well, I sat there at that desk, and feelings swam into my consciousness of my heritage of fathers: . . . and "father beyond father beyond father"[8]—my own father, my grandfather, my great-grandfather. There at the graveside in the Oakwood Cemetery, was the modest headstone reading, ROBERT BIELBY RAINES, singer of hymns, like my Dad, like me . . . and if you go back far enough through the continuities of Methodist history, like Charles Wesley. It was some of his hymns—"Love Divine," "O For a Thousand Tongues," "Hark the Herald Angels Sing"—that we all loved especially. Charles Wesley in my singing heart. Still sweeping.

In March the following year, my son Bob went with his church choir on a singing swing of west coast Florida churches. While there he wrote me:

Dear Dad,
So much to tell you about Florida . . . sun out every day except for one . . . I got intensely tan . . . the waves on the beaches were large, so I dove, frolicked and body-surfed on/in the waves . . . on the third day of the trip we did our first performance. It turned out really well. Mr. Jenkins [the choir director] had me do the worship service afterwards, and I read Scripture, read a story, and prayed. I did an excellent job and received many a hug. There were about two hundred people at the performance, many of whom knew Grandpa and some of whom knew you. Throughout the trip I was constantly reminded of my heritage by

ministers and other people. I was one of the wise men
in the play . . . danced and sang with two others . . .
had a few solo lines, too. The three kings' number was
the comic relief in the show, always receiving the
largest applause by the delighted audience. The
older people seemed particularly touched. They
often cried and laughed. So many comments on my
similar speech and mannerisms with yours. It was a
joy spreading The Word to such receptive audiences.

Another singing sweeper! And son after son after
son. . . .

There is a black cabinet in the garage at Glen Lake.
While rummaging through it that summer, I came across
four bundles of letters, with my name on one and my
siblings' names on the others. They were letters each of us
had written to Mother and Dad from our earliest
childhood. Dad saved them and added carbon copies of
some letters he had written to us when he was at his office.
He wrote us almost weekly. In saving and preserving
these letters, he was giving us the gift of yesterday.
Waiting there—the black cabinet—for our interest to
awaken. I came upon one undated letter, written on
Camp Lincoln stationery. We children all spent a few
weeks every summer at this camp in northern Minnesota.
This particular letter was written when I was about eight
years old; if so, 1934, and was sent to my parents who
were vacationing in Florida at the time . . .

Dear Mother and Dad,
I have just put down my Bible so I thought I'd write
you a letter as the Bible reminded me of you. Here
are three of the verses:

God is our refuge and our strength
A very present help in trouble
Therefore we will not fear though the
    earth change
And though mountains be shaken into the
    heart of the seas;
Though the waters thereof roar and be
    troubled
Though the mountains tremble with the
    swelling thereof.
            Selah.
Psalms 46
Verses 1, 2, 3
That is just a bit, but the verse where the waters roar
reminded me of you near the floods.

(There was flooding in the area of Florida where they
were staying.) From childhood I became an incorrigibly
biblical person, needing and wanting to resonate my life
choices against biblical narratives and persons, and
trying to recognize myself in biblical stories.

I feared it would be sad that summer up there at Glen
Lake. And it was—sometimes. But a peacefulness was
there as well. I sat one day alone in the Last Resort, in
Dad's chair by the big window, where he would sit with a
piece of plaster board on his lap, writing his letters by
hand. I felt a healing of some dis-ease and a flood of
gratitude—gratitude for my parents and to them—
gratitude to God. I have second and third thoughts
about some things I said to my folks or didn't say, and I
find it a strange grace that their deaths should release
gratitude that wasn't fully available to express before

their deaths. But it's all there in the communion of saints—and somehow gathered up.

Dietrich Bonhoeffer wrote from his cell in a Nazi prison, "For the past week or two these words have been constantly running through my head, 'Let pass, dear brother, every pain; what lacketh you I'll bring again.' What does 'bring again' mean? It means that nothing is lost, everything is taken up again in Christ ... transfigured in the process, becoming transparent, clear and free from all self-seeking. . . . Christ brings it all again as God intended it to be. . . . The doctrine of the restoration of all things—derived from Ephesians 1:10, is a magnificent conception and full of comfort."[9]

So it is. Now and then I can allow myself to sink into its gentle, strong flow.

On July 14, 1980, my parents were to celebrate their sixtieth wedding anniversary. And, of course, it was being celebrated at Glen Lake. Several years before, my father lost his wedding ring somewhere on the grounds around the cottages. Thorough searching failed to uncover it, so another ring was purchased. That July in 1980, my eleven-year-old stepson Matthew was playing by the swing about the Last Resort. He saw something glistening on the ground. He picked up a gold ring and brought it to his mother. Inside its worn surface, we read, "July 14, 1920." My Father's lost wedding ring! Matt was somewhat reluctantly persuaded to keep the secret until the anniversary celebration five days hence. My parents could scarcely believe the serendipity of the lost and found ring in the sixtieth year of their marriage. All of us wondered about the marvelous synchronicity of a child at play who found such a treasure hidden underfoot in the soil of the years. None of us could know that just over a year later, both Mother and Dad would be gone.

One hot morning during the summer of 1982, we put up the green shade on the north side of the Big Cottage. A fresh breeze wafted in, and we realized that we could see a northern corner of the lake hidden from view when the shade was down, not to mention the lofty branches of the big evergreens towering over the Last Resort. We went about our daily tasks, closed up the porch doors at evening as it got cool, and the next morning came out on the porch, coffee in hand, and saw a new and spacious scene. The shade was up. And it was all right. The shade stayed up. There was that spontaneity of spiritual space now peaceful, glad— without monitoring, with communion. Thank God. The circle was turning.

2
The Turning Circle

In the months that followed, I found there was a heaviness growing within me and sorrow lying in my soul. What was it? I knew that it was more than grieving the death of my father.

I had begun reading the *New Yorker* articles by Jonathan Schell, which were eventually published as the book *The Fate of the Earth*. Schell's writing caused me to imagine and feel the horror of nuclear war in a more comprehensive and profound way than before. He makes the distinction between death, which is the end of *life,* and extinction, which is the end of *birth.* He notes that the prospect of extinction gives everyday life in the nuclear world a cast of coldness, bitterness, despair; that in order to live fully human lives, we have to feel our connections with the generations that came before us and those that will follow; that in imagining extinction, "We are left only with the ghostlike cancelled future generations, who, metaphorically speaking, have been waiting through all past time to enter into life but have now been turned back by us."[1]

I had always imagined the cloud of witnesses as those who have gone before us, now including my own parents. Schell was making me feel the anguish of the cloud of witnesses yearning to come after us, including our children and grandchildren, nieces and nephews, and all the little ones . . . even the unborn billions patiently waiting their turn. On my fifty-fourth birthday, my daughter Nancy said to me, "Daddy, I wish I believed I will live to be fifty-four." Nancy is a dancer who lives in New York City. She thinks a nuclear war in her lifetime is likely and that she will not survive it. One day I realized that my four children and two step-children all live in missile targets—that Russian missiles are aimed at them right now.

The generations are rolling over. The turning of the human season is upon us. As I work on the material and spiritual legacy of my parents to me and my siblings, I find myself wondering about my legacy to my children. As I sweep up the heart and hearth of the unfinished business of my parents' lives, I stumble upon unfinished business in my own life. Things to do, relationships to restore, attention to be paid, reconnections to be made, while there is yet time. The cloud of witnesses before us causes us to look over our shoulders at the cloud of witnesses coming after us, lest they be denied by another—a mushroom cloud.

Death lifts the shades of our houses and the lids of the eyes of our hearts (Eph. 1:18) to see what we didn't, couldn't, see before. I see my father's righteous nose and know I am lonely for him while still vexed with him. Other people feel even more strongly torn.

Even as I feel my father's hands gently rubbing my back, I have a fierce body-longing for my son. I want these physical connections to hold, not to fade, not to leak out of my memory, diminishing my hope. I *need* to hold hands across the generational cloud of witnesses, and not to lose touch either way. It's difficult for me to talk with my children about the danger of nuclear war, and its threat to their future. There they go eagerly, joyously living their lives, singing in choirs, buying houses, planning families, building careers, following their dreams. How do you talk to your children about the amputation of their future?

Schell writes,

> Formerly, the future was simply given to us; now it must be achieved. We must become the agriculturalists of time. . . . In asking us to cherish the lives of the unborn, the peril of extinction takes us back to the ancient principle of the sacredness of human life, but it conducts us there by a new path. Instead of being asked not to kill our neighbors, we are asked to let them be born. . . . If the ideal for the relationship among living people is brotherhood, then the ideal for the relationship of the living to the unborn is parenthood. Universal brotherhood, which seeks to safeguard lives that are already in existence, embodies the solicitude and protectiveness of love, and its highest command, therefore, is "Thou shalt not kill." Universal parenthood, which would seek to bring life into existence out of nothing, would embody the creativity and abundant generosity of love, and its highest commandment, therefore, would be, "Be fruitful and multiply." But this commandment is not the strictly biological one. The nuclear peril makes all of us, whether we happen to have children of our own or not, the parents of all future generations. . . . every generation that holds the earth hostage to nuclear destruction holds a gun to the head of its own children.[2]

The circle is turning, and I am turning inside it, over and around and over again. I am a son and I am a father. There is a "before" and an "after" that runs through me. While I am wanting to say to my parents,

"Thank you, I love you, I forgive you, forgive me," I am also wanting to say to my children, "Bless you, I love you, forgive me, I forgive you." This revolving door of parenting and being parented is both comforting and confusing.

Herbert Tarr gives us a poignant picture of the turning circle.

The conductor called, . . . "All visitors off the train!" "Oh David . . ." She hugged him to her bosom which smelled of fruits and vegetables and a mother's love. "Take care of him." These last words were addressed not to Uncle Asher nor even to the conductor, but to God. Tante Dvorah spoke to Him freely and often, for the Lord, to her way of thinking, was a person-sitter to whom loved ones were safely to be entrusted, as well as her senior partner in the business of living, always accessible and invariably amenable to petitions of love.

David looked at his aunt and uncle—she, with hands chapped and hard from selling fruit and vegetables outdoors in all kinds of weather, the face ruddy and round and invariably smiling, the heavy body more accustomed to half a dozen sweaters at one time than a single coat, the hair the color of moonlight now, but the dark eyes still bright; he, with his slight wiry body strong and bent from lifting too many fruit and vegetable crates for too many years, the wind-burned skin, the swarthy face impassive except for the wry mouth—the childless couple who had taken the orphaned David into their home, rearing him since the age of seven, yet refusing to be called "Mama" and "Papa" for fear that he would forget his real parents.

David grabbed their rough peddlers' hands in his smooth student ones. "How can I ever begin to repay you two for what you've done for me!" Uncle Asher spoke

gently: "David, there's a saying: 'The love of parents goes
to their children, but the love of these parents goes to
their children.' "

"That's not so!" David protested. "I'll always be trying
to"—Tante Dvorah interrupted. "David, what your Uncle
Asher means is that a parent's love isn't to be paid back; it
can only be passed on."[3]

I am struck by the recurring resonance of the
vocation of *parenthood* as a way to speak of preserving
the world for coming generations. We feel it personally
for our own children. One picture of a Vietnamese girl
running down a street, her back flaming with napalm,
made us feel it for all the children of Vietnam. One
child of Hiroshima, her flesh peeling off her abdomen,
makes us feel it for all the victims of that bomb, and all
the bombs that have fallen, and may yet fall. We are a
post-holocaust generation, and also perhaps a pre-holo-
caust generation. We are in between, with a vocation of
universal parenthood, which we share not only with
other human beings but with the entire creation, as it
groans with us in travail for a new creation to be born
(Rom. 8:22).

Mary Bateson writes, "If we meditate on the future of
an individual child, we must gradually embrace the
whole human community and the whole biosphere of
our planet . . . This environment is a vast collaboration,
a dance of co-parenting by air and water and sun and
moon; by bacteria and plants and other living creatures;
by other people. Even, in the end, by other nations . . .
as nice as the Russians are to their children, their
children live because we don't blow them up. We are the
only people who can look after the children in Russia.
And vice versa."[4]

Part of my ambivalence was this gnawing sorrow in my soul for the future of all the children. But there was something else. Something to do with what Erik Erikson calls the tension between "generativity" and "stagnation," the central psychological and spiritual struggle going on in our souls at midlife. He writes that:

> Generativity is primarily the interest in establishing and guiding the next generation, although there are people who, from misfortune, or because of special and genuine gifts in other directions, do not apply this drive to offspring but to other forms of altruistic concern and of creativity, which may absorb their kind of parental responsibility. . . . Individuals who do not develop generativity, often begin to indulge themselves as if they were their own one and only child.[5]

The options: exercise parental responsibility, i.e., care, towards tomorrow, or curl up in one's own narrowing circle today. He states, "Care is a quality essential for psychosocial evolution, for we are the teaching species. . . . Once we have grasped this interlocking of the human life stages, we understand that adult man is so constituted as to *need to be needed* lest he suffer the mental deformation of self-absorption, in which he becomes his own infant and pet. . . . *Care is the widening concern for what has been generated by love, necessity or accident; it overcomes the ambivalence adhering to irreversible obligation.*"[6]

Take care. But sometimes I just don't care. Part of me doesn't want to see one more suffering child's face, wants to hide away in these hills, wants to enjoy my wife and friends and creatures of this mountainside and my own solitude. Another part of me, or perhaps the same part, won't let me do it carelessly, carefreely. Though

my personal journey of the past several years has strewn
my path with breakage and left me and others with costs
yet to be paid, still I am a whistler. While I work, while I
walk in the woods, when I come into the office, or so I'm
told, I whistle. A nose-stroker and a whistler. If I'm not
careful, I have lots of positive thoughts.

My natural response to the idea of the generativity-
stagnation polarity is that, of course, I am marked for
generativity. So I must hurry to experience it, leaving
stagnation for other less fortunate (less worthy?) folk to
suffer. I am learning more about soul, about my soul,
and why I have lately suffered "weakness" of soul.
Marie-Louise von Franz writes of:

> The phenomenon of "loss of soul" . . . there is the fear
> that someone who has died may take the soul of someone
> close to him along with him into the realm of the dead
> . . . "Loss of soul" appears in the form of the sudden
> onset of apathy and listlessness; the joy has gone out of
> life, initiative is crippled, one feels empty, everything
> seems pointless. Close observation, especially of dreams,
> will reveal that a large part of the psychic energy has
> flowed off into the unconscious and is, therefore, no
> longer at the disposal of the ego . . . If one perseveres
> long enough in this condition, in most cases . . . an
> intense new interest in life emerges, an interest that now
> strives in a direction different from the previous
> one. . . . One can observe beneath the crippling stagna-
> tion of the personality an especially intense desire of
> some sort . . . which the depressed patient, however,
> does not . . . dare to allow to come to the surface.[7]

I don't pretend to understand this theory, but it does
intrigue me, and yields two insights of value. One is that
my preoccupation with sweeping up the heart and

hearth of my parents' lives—a task still unfinished—and my yearning after them to reweave threads of our relationships that were left hanging, have resulted in some "loss of soul," some descent of psychic energy into the unconscious for work that needs to be done there. But, in the meantime, I am left here on the surface—dry, apathetic, neither hot nor cold, comme çi, comme ça, ambivalent.

The second insight is that I am now beginning to experience some restoration or recovery of soul, a fresh energy rising within me, whose new direction is not yet manifest. Endings and beginnings are being integrated; grieving and birthing are in the process of healing me.

Carl Jung further amplifies the loss and recovery of soul when he writes that we embark upon the second half of life . . .

> With the false assumption that our truths and ideals will serve us as hitherto. But we cannot live the afternoon of life according to the programme of life's morning: for what was great in the morning will be little at evening, and what in the morning was true will at evening have become a lie . . . For a young person it is almost a sin, or at least a danger, to be too preoccupied with himself; but for the ageing person it is a duty and a necessity to devote serious attention to himself. . . . The afternoon of human life must also have a significance of its own, and cannot be merely a pitiful appendage to life's morning. The significance of the morning undoubtedly lies in the development of the individual, our entrenchment in the outer world, the propagation of our kind, and the care of our children. This is the obvious purpose of nature. But when this purpose has been attained . . . shall the earning of money, the extension of conquests, and the expansion of life go steadily on

beyond the bounds of all reason and sense? Whoever
carries over into the afternoon the law of the morning
. . . must pay for it with damage to his soul.[8]

No one makes it into middle age without a damaged
soul. And that's not all bad. When a friend of Jung told
him that he had just had a promotion, Jung offered his
condolences, saying to his friend that he would stop
growing for a time. James Hillman says that soul is
connected with the underside, not with up or white or
light, but down, dark, grief, failure, woundedness,
sickness. Robert Bly notes that if you're a preacher,
poet, businessman, artist, teacher, whatever, and you
do it very well, chances are your soul is not in it, because
"performance escapes soul." What do we make of this?
There is craft and its discipline. There is art and its
expression. There is performance, which is the visible
embodiment of the soul of the artist in material or
movement. Maybe when one forgets oneself in the
performance, soul is in it, but when one thinks in the
midst of the performance how well one is doing, soul
has just died.

In Walker Percy's novel *The Second Coming*, Will
Barrett's wife Marion has just died. When Jack Curl, the
priest of their Episcopal church comes to see him, Will
thinks about Jack:

How could he not have noticed this about Jack Curl
before? That even as he was moving his shoulders
around under his jump suit, playing the sweaty
clergyman doing good, that Jack too was trying to catch
hold of his own life? that in the very moment of this
joking godly confrontation—sure, I'm trying to con you
out of three million, Will, but it's a good cause and I'm

> God's own con man, okay? and so forth—here was Jack
> Curl trying to catch hold. And wasn't he doing it? Wasn't
> he doing everything right? Yet when you took a good
> look at him, this sweaty Episcopal handyman, this godly
> greasy super, you saw in an instant that he was not quite
> there. Looking at him was like trying to focus on a
> blurred photograph.[9]

A blurred soul. A soul out of focus. My soul may be
coming into focus again—"say the word and my soul
shall be healed"—as my strength of soul has lately
increased, a seemingly fruitless time has proven also to
have been a fallow time. There is fresh energy towards
tomorrow, and a letting go of some things, including a
thirty-six-year-old typewriter.

When I went away to college in 1946, my parents gave
me a Royal portable typewriter. It was, of course, a
manual typewriter. I have used it ever since. In
November of 1982, I bought an electric typewriter.
How is it that I could have waited thirty-six years to get a
new typewriter? I have needed one for years. The "G"
key was almost entirely obliterated. I have gotten used
to pounding the keys. I have trouble trying to develop a
lighter touch as I experiment with the new typewriter,
although I am still learning not to be heavy-handed in
other areas of my life. Cindy notes that I am speaking
less of my parents now than a few months ago. Perhaps
I am allowing them to take their proper place in the
communion of the saints, and going about the business
of my own life, with no less gratitude or appreciation,
but less preoccupation, an appropriate flow of energy to
the "afternoon" tasks of my life.

I find myself in the Elijah story, which has become a

paradigm for me. When Elijah goes on the run from
Jezebel and finally makes it to Mount Horeb, he takes
refuge in a cave. He hears the sounds of earthquake,
wind, and fire, but the Lord's voice is not in any of them.
He moves to the mouth of the cave, the border of safety
and vulnerability. Then he hears a still, small voice . . .
asking, "What are you doing here, Elijah?" (I Kings
19:9). It is a question of vocation. After Elijah makes his
excuses, the Lord's question becomes a command: to
get out of the cave, go back to his home scene, anoint
new religious and political leaders, and retire.

When I sit in the crow's nest of this mountain
sanctuary, and hear that question, "What are you doing
here, Bob?" it is also, for me, a question of vocation.
How is it that after more than nine years, I am still here
on the edge of sanctuary, welcoming people to the
mouth of the cave?

Sometimes I wake in the night, amazed that I am out
here in the boonies (Kirkridge) and fear that the action
is over there somewhere, where there are cities and lots
of people. But then, in grace, I remember that God's
action takes place among people and in human hearts
here as elsewhere, that every place is equidistant from
grace, and every time may be kairos.

Who would have thought, two thousand years ago,
that God was acting not only in Rome, but also (and
especially) in that backwater town, Nazareth, on the
edge of empire? But more pertinent perhaps for me is
the truth that I feel called to be a keeper of hearth and
hospitality here. I really would rather be a doorkeeper
in *this* house of the Lord than be something else. It's not
just the "goodness of fit" between myself and my life
structure that enables who I am to be in harmony with

what I'm doing. Nor is it just the privilege of having orchestra seats for hearing and beholding the still, sad, noisy, joyous music of humanity playing before me—close up, close in. It is also the fun of helping to shape this little institution into a golden cone of the Lord, a circle of networking and intersection, a zone of transformation.

Surely, one is lucky and blessed when one's job slips over one's vocation like a comfortable old corduroy jacket over the shoulders. Holy vestments.

A job may be comfortable for a time. But vocation yanks me out of comfort. I feel the obligation to pass on my love. I keep hearing the cries of the children. Morris West's novel *The Clowns of God* is set in Europe in the 1990s. Professor Mendelius and his daughter, Katrin, talk together about her intention to live with her lover, but not get married. He asks her why they don't want to get married. And she responds,

> "I'm afraid; we're both afraid."
> "Of what?"
> "Of always . . . just that. Of getting married and having children and trying to make a home, while the whole world could tumble around our ears in a day."
> Suddenly she was passionate and eloquent, "You older ones don't understand. You've survived a war. You've built things. You've had us. We're grown up. But look at the world you've left us! All along the borders there are rocket launchers and missile silos . . . You've given us everything except tomorrow!"[10]

More than anything, we want to give our children, grandchildren, nieces, nephews, and all the little ones, including the unborn, the gift of tomorrow. It is our

deepest vocation, our most holy life work. William
Stringfellow understands vocation as the name for the
discernment of the coincidence of the Word of God in
history with one's own selfhood. He reflects on the
death of his friend and colleague, Anthony Towne, "I
realized that Anthony's death raised the matter of my
vocation once more, in an abrupt, radical, awful,
perchance final way."[11]

We realize that the deaths of those close to us and all
the little and large deaths of our lives, and Death
waiting for us in the bomb, have raised the matter of our
vocation once more, in an abrupt, radical, awful,
perchance final way.

In the spring of 1983, our friend David wrote about
his preparations for brain surgery, an operation that
could prove fatal.

> I am feeling that my life belongs to others as much as it
> belongs to me and I am in a wonderful period of sharing
> and inquiry. It is so interesting . . . I now am able to
> clearly identify the persons who love me and I love. I find
> I am talking, strongly, with these persons about
> "gifts"—theirs and mine. And, when the sharing is
> finished, I find, not loneliness about "why I should be
> with such affliction," but rather I find a deep solitude
> where I am about the work of discovering the voice that
> tells me about my inner necessity—that is, my vocation
> . . . As I pray, for clarity, for the discovery of the center
> of my life in my own heart, and for the ways I might fully
> express my gifts both before and after the surgery, I have
> noticed that I am praying for healing—but not so much
> for myself as for others. I see *so clearly now* the hurt and
> pain in this world and feel such compassion for those
> around me who are suffering and crippled in mind or

spirit—for the thousands upon thousands who are hurting. I pray for their healing with a new intensity now and I invite you to remember all these brothers and sisters as you continue to pray for my healing.

When the energy of inner necessity yields clarity in the center of the soul, ambivalence gives birth to vocation.

3
By the Skin of Our Eyes

On Sunday, August 8, 1982, I stood in a small gathering of people outside the Monroe County Court House in Stroudsburg, Pennsylvania. Stroudsburg is five miles from Kirkridge. I was participating for the first time in a public witness of Hiroshima Memorial Day. It was the first such public remembrance in Stroudsburg. We were speaking in the town square of that unspeakable day, August 6, 1945, when the first atomic bomb was dropped on human beings. On that day in 1945 I was at the naval base Treasure Island in California. Within weeks I would be on a troop ship headed for the Philippine Islands; in fact, to a Seabee base on the island of Samar. I was nineteen years old, having enlisted in the Navy in July 1944, upon graduation from high school. Boot camp at Great Lakes, training schools at Texas A. & M. and Navy Pier in Chicago; learning to be a radar and sonar technician. I had enlisted at age eighteen, with nary a conscientious-objecting thought. Hitler was threatening the life of western civilization. He seemed to be the very incarnation of evil, and there was nothing for it but to fight against Germany, Japan, and Italy—winning, saving the world from barbarism. Or so it seemed. VE day came on May 7, 1945, and now in August we were preparing to go for the great and terrible island-hopping invasion of Japan itself.

On August 6, at 8:15 A.M., a fission bomb with a yield of 12.5 kilotons was detonated nineteen hundred feet above the central section of the city of Hiroshima. Within a matter of seconds, that city of three hundred and forty thousand persons became a cauldron of fire. Ninety thousand people died in the initial seconds— vaporized, crushed, burned to ash instantly . . . ashen shadows left where a moment before a man or woman or child had been. Other tens of thousands died in the weeks that followed—of radiation sickness, burns, diseases. Hiroshima victims are still dying in 1983 as I write, and will be dying for years to come. A placard at the entrance of the Peace Memorial Museum in Hiroshima reads: "The museum hopes to speak on behalf of 200,000 victims' voiceless voices, the witness of history."

President Truman told the nation and world about the bomb dropped on Hiroshima the next day. He said, "We have spent more than two billion on the greatest scientific gamble in history—and we have won. Having found the atomic bomb, we shall use it. We shall continue to use it on city after city. . . . We thank God it has come to us . . . and we pray that he may guide us to use it in his ways and for his purposes."

My Navy buddies and I were jubilant. Japan had surrendered. The war was over. Though we would still spend nearly a year in the Philippines, we would be safe, and home, sooner than we had dreamed possible. Nobody that I knew of asked what it could mean to use the atomic bomb in God's ways and for God's purposes. Nobody I knew wondered how the burning up of over one hundred thousand human beings at once could serve the purpose of a loving God.

So, thirty-seven years later, a few of us stood outside the Monroe County Court House, asking that question. It has taken me nearly thirty-seven years to begin to understand that history took a fateful turning on that August 1945 day, a turning that will lead either to the end of all wars or to the end of the world. Most nations observe their own particular Memorial Day to honor the dead of their nation's wars, just as we celebrate May 30 in this country. The most important memorial day in human history has now become this Human Memorial Day, to be acknowledged, remembered, and confessed year by year.

Hiroshima-Nagasaki is a searing, bleeding photo of what our world can become any half-hour from now. To bring this image closer to home, if a one megaton bomb (small by today's standards) were dropped on New York City, among the millions taken up into the mushroom cloud would be my twenty-three-year-old daughter Nancy. If a bomb were dropped on Chicago, among the ashen-shadow memories would be my twenty-eight-year-old daughter Cathy and her husband, Mike. If a bomb were dropped on Columbus, Ohio, the charred victims would include my seventeen-year-old son Bob and twenty-six-year-old daughter Barbara, and step-children Sally, twenty, and Matt, thirteen. My story is your story. It is the human story.

Schell's *The Fate Of The Earth,* like Rachel Carson's *Silent Spring* of twenty years ago, alerts us to the growing possibility of a silent *earth*—a possible result of an all-out nuclear war is the erosion of the earth's ozone layer, which shields us from the lethal rays of the sun. Schell writes, "The common world . . . is made up of all institutions, all cities, nations, and other communities, and all works of fabrication, art, thought and science, and it survives the death of every individual. It is basic to the common world that it encompasses not only the present but all past and future generations."[1] It is this common world or commonwealth that is now in danger of extinction by threat of nuclear arms.

Two days before our gathering outside the Monroe County Court House on August 6, 1982, the literal thirty-seventh anniversary of the Hiroshima bombing, the Department of Energy with stunning insensitivity detonated an underground nuclear explosion. Secretary of Energy James Edwards was there to observe a two hundred feet deep hole ripped out of the bowels of the earth. He found it "exciting," and said, "I hope we don't have nuclear war . . . but if we do, we don't want to come out #2."[2]

"We are Number 1" may be a mentality that still has merit on the football field, but it is now, in the common world, a dinosaur mentality. We all know what happened to the dinosaurs. We are learning that there is no "either/or" way of survival for nations, but only a "both-and" way. The golden rule is no longer, if it ever was, a private option, but has become a political necessity. Do unto other nations what you would that they should do unto you. We are now locked together with the Russians in a new kind of nuclear family, from which there will never ever again be any escape. Like it or not, like them or not, like us or not . . . we and they live together or die together. It is win-win or lose-lose.

By the terrible irony of the gift of cosmic power available on this tiny planet for good or ill, God has opened to us a way of life or a way of death—which we must choose. We are required to choose. Daily we are choosing. Nuclear disarmament—mutual bilateral nuclear disarmament—is the consummate issue that connects and grounds all other issues and gives them their relevance. Either we find ways to solve this question or everything will quite literally go up in smoke.

We live now in the era of the seventh beatitude. "Blessed are the peacemakers, for they shall be called [the children] of God" (Matt. 5:9). That innocent, gentle blessing, lying there in the pages of the New Testament for nearly two thousand years, repeated to and by Sunday school children century after century, in country after country, has been innocuously privatized to personal relationships. But now, post-Hiroshima, it flashes with an alternating green light/red light. It is *the* beatitude of the human era. Blessed are the peacemakers, for they shall be called the caretakers of creation, the protectors of the children of God.

One morning not long ago, I was preparing a Bible study for a group of clergy and laity who were exploring peacemaking in their parishes. I was meditating on the familiar passage from Psalm 34:14, "Depart from evil, and do good; seek peace, and pursue it." As I mulled the matter of pursuing peace, I realized that Peace had been pursuing me all these years. Something had been happening to and in me, as to a whole generation of us. It reminded me of an episode in the film, *The Horse's Mouth*. The film tells the story of a bohemian painter who lives on a houseboat. In one scene a young admirer of the artist asks him why and how he became a painter. The man looks out through the broken window as though at something far away and says, "One time I saw a painting by Matisse. I was stunned and suddenly saw

the world in color, as though for the first time. He
skinned my eyes; I became a different man; it was like a
conversion."

How did many of us become peacemakers? It *has*
been like a conversion, a slow skinning of my eyes. Peace
has been skinning my eyes, and perhaps yours too. I am
beginning to see the world in the color of peace. The
skinning began on the island of Samar where I first
heard the term *gook* used to refer to the Filippino
people. I watched the lines of GI's waiting in line for a
few minutes with a teen-age Filippino girl, turned
whore by our military presence. I saw the contempt
many of my comrades had for these Asians, these
gooks, and although my own feelings were mixed, and I
felt some sadness and outrage for them, I did not say
anything or do anything. I did not make the connection
then, but later I would understand why it was easier for
Americans to accept the atomic bombing of Hiroshima
and Nagasaki—they were Japanese cities, populated
with oriental people, one kind or another of gook. In
1942, it was just as acceptable for President Roosevelt to
intern thousands of Japanese-Americans on the West
Coast, without protest from the American people—just
as I would remember in the Vietnam war years the
primary GI term for the Vietnamese—*gooks.*

The skinning of my eyes continued as the Vietnam
war heated up in the 1960s. Gladys Barkman was a
member of First United Methodist Church of Germantown in Philadelphia, where I was a minister in those
years. She and I belonged to a koinonia group that had
been meeting for several years. She was a longtime
pacifist and member of the Women's International
League for Peace and Freedom. I had never heard of it,

though it was founded in 1915 and has offered a continuous witness for peace to the present day. Gladys got me to join her on a march down Philadelphia streets one Sunday afternoon in the spring of 1965. I don't remember the specific issue being marched about, but it was my first time on the streets for peace. Civil rights preoccupied us in those years, and it would be awhile before the connections were made between peace-making and civil rights, as in Martin Luther King, Jr.'s Riverside Church address in 1967. Once again, as I write in the spring of 1983, these connections are being made toward the August 1983 "Jobs, Peace, Freedom" demonstration in Washington. Gladys was my first skinner.

A photo album of my Being-Pursued-By-Peace pilgrimage would include:

—A picture of my daughter Cathy, fourteen years old, carrying an American flag in a peace demonstration in Washington in 1968.

—My view from a bus of peace people from Philadelphia who flashed the peace sign of two fingers to a row of policemen—several grinned and flashed it back.

—I am swaying in a crowd of 250,000 jammed into the mall between the Lincoln Memorial and the Washington Monument, singing along with Pete Seeger, "All we are asking, is . . . give peace a chance . . . give peace a chance" flowing like a rolling river of hope.

—The headline in the *Columbus Citizen-Journal*, the Tuesday before Christmas Sunday in 1972: "Bombs Send Peace Message to Hanoi," the Christmas bombing. Anguish, anger, and a sermon that caused an uproar in the congregation in First Community Church, Columbus, Ohio.

—Happenings at Kent State, Ohio State, Jackson State.

—Working with the deacons of First Community Church to publish a statement of support for those refusing the draft on the basis of conscientious objection as well as those choosing to be drafted.

(These were common photos in the Americana albums of those years.)

And then to Kirkridge in 1974: a divorce, a resignation from one job, a remarriage, accepting another job. Grieving and birthing to do. Healing to do and to let happen, personal sabbath time and space, while seeking to develop this small institution. While we worked, planned, fought, prayed, and struggled, and through it all were being healed and gaining strength of soul, the skinning of our eyes went on.

The arms race was heating up in the late 1970s. Daniel Berrigan led his first retreat on peacemaking at Kirkridge in November 1978, thus beginning, though we did not know it, the major ongoing surgery of our sight. The Riverside Church Disarmament Program, World Peacemakers, Sojourners, Jonah House, and other groups and individuals resourced, encouraged and made pilgrimage with us. We became aware of the Physicians for Social Responsibility. Maps began to appear in newspapers all across the country showing in graphic detail what would happen to that city should a one megaton bomb be dropped on it. I was surprised during a 1980 winter visit to my folks in Lakeland, Florida, to see such a map in the Lakeland paper while I was there. Many people were getting their eyes skinned. It was painful and confusing.

In recent years, we have watched the obscene militarization of our society—the sorrow and waste of many of the best of our young scientists and engineers who have little option but to work one way or another for the military, while unemployment increased to double digits, and resources were taken from the poor, the dispossessed, and the elderly—40 percent of the black teen-agers were unable to find work, and so on and on and on. This skinning was painful surgery.

Then came two events in 1980 that took more skin. The people of Jonah House in Baltimore organized a daily presence and witness at the Pentagon through the year of 1980. The idea was to have people at the doors of the Pentagon every day for that entire calendar year. They invited friends and groups across the country to take a week, and people came.

Kirkridge took the major part of a week in late April. The Kirkridge Seven included my wife Cindy, Betty Jane Ricker—a Kirkridge Board Member from Montclair, N.J.—Steve Hooper and Matt Smith from Cornell University, Evelyn Spacarelli from Philadelphia, Herb Frey, a Presbyterian pastor in Wilkes-Barre, and me. Cindy, long a banner-maker, made a special one for this event. It has a white dove above rainbow stripes, with a Celtic cross at the bottom. In later years, as that beautiful banner found its way to Groton, the Norristown jail, Stroudsburg, Allentown, New York City, and various other places, the name Kirkridge was added along the bottom.

Our group stayed, as did the other groups, on the second floor (and I mean "floor" quite literally) of St.

Stephen's and the Incarnation Episcopal Church in Washington, D.C. This church has long had a ministry to the poor and provided hospitality to peacemakers and war resisters. We happened to be there over the weekend during which preparations were being made for the civil disobedience that was to take place on the Pentagon steps on Monday, April 28. While most of the witnessing was distributing leaflets, street theater, standing with posters, talking with passers-by—whatever each group worked out—April 28 was a day for civil disobedience.

Al Zook, a gentle, passionate member of the Church of the Brethren, was our group coordinator. Molly Rush helped us all prepare. John Schuchardt had coordinated Monday's planning with other organizations. The sit-in began to take place; blood was thrown on the sand-gray pillars by some of our friends. Arrests were made. Daniel Ellsberg, Benjamin Spock, and Phil Berrigan were among scores arrested.

The Kirkridge people were part of an affinity group for some of our Jonah House friends. Our responsibility was to track them, find out where they were jailed, and go there and help in whatever ways we could. So I found myself in the county jail in Alexandria, Virginia, visiting Liz McAllister and her two children Jerry and Freda, who needed cookies and oranges. I saw Al, Phil, John, and others. The implacable death-gray Pentagon and the power of the State . . . the gospel witness of friends, willing to risk jail for their faith, and for the children of the world—they all worked on me and in me.

While I have taken what I regard as difficult and costly steps in my private and professional life because of my political witness, I usually have calculated my costs and kept them low. While I have been arrested, I have not yet spent a night in jail. Fear, dislike of discomfort, competing responsibilites, etc., etc. . . . These Jonah House people called my timidity into question, or more accurately, my being with them called it into question. The Kirkridge Seven came home roused, wanting to commit ourselves and Kirkridge to a deeper, more serious, level of peacemaking. We had the summer to mull it over—and then something else happened.

On September 9, 1980, at 6:50 A.M. eight persons slipped by guards into the General Electric plant in King of Prussia, Pennsylvania. (This plant made the Mark 12A first strike reentry vehicle, intended for Minuteman III and Trident II. One warhead can produce ninety Hiroshimas.) The eight took hammers and beat on the missile cone heads, literally trying to "beat swords into plowshares." The action involved *minor property* damage as a way of dramatizing the *major human* damage being readied by the war machine today. The action was in the tradition of Jesus, who also did minor property damage when he overturned the Temple tables as a way of dramatizing the major human damage being perpetrated by the Temple system of the time.

The Plowshares Eight, as they came to be called, identified their purpose in a newsletter to friends:

SWORDS INTO PLOWSHARES

The prophets Isaiah and Micah summon us to beat "swords into plowshares." Therefore eight of us from the Atlantic Life Community come to King of Prussia

G.E. Re-entry Plant to expose the criminality of nuclear weaponry and corporate piracy. We represent resistance communities along the east coast; each of us has a long history of *non-violent resistance to war*.

We commit civil disobedience at G.E. because this genocidal entity is the fifth leading producer of weaponry in the U.S. To maintain this position, G.E. drains $3 million a day from the public treasury—an enormous larceny against the poor. We wish to challenge the lethal lies done by G.E. through its motto, *"WE BRING GOOD THINGS TO LIFE."* As manufacturer of the Mark 12A re-entry vehicle, G.E. actually prepares to bring good things to death. Through the Mark 12A, the threat of first strike nuclear war grows more eminent. Thus G.E. advances the possible destruction of millions of innocent lives.

In confronting G.E., we choose to obey God's law of life rather than a corporate summons to death. Our "beating of swords into plowshares" today is a way to enflesh this biblical call. In our action we draw on a deep-rooted faith in Christ who changed the course of history through his willingness to suffer rather than to kill. We are filled with hope for our world and for our children as we join this act of resistance.

On October 29 I visited five of the men who were being held in the Montgomery County Jail in Norristown, Pennsylvania. Dressed in prison blue, they spoke of daily Bible study, opportunities to help other prisoners in legal and personal ways, spiritual preparations for trial, sentencing, and the possibility of years in prison. Their faces radiated a quiet joy. I brought a

small bit of cash for coffee and stamps—and a large cup
of love from Kirkridge friends.

Later that fall Daniel Berrigan, out on bail for
medical reasons, led a retreat at Kirkridge on the theme
Election and Vocation. Insights abounded:

> The Christian Gospel is indictable by the State. . . . If
> Christ, not America, tells us who we are, where we come
> from, and where we are to go, we are anarchic to the
> State. . . . salvation is found today by most people in the
> State. . . . the bomb is our security, our savior, our
> salvation. . . . in order to 'protect' our security we will do
> literally anything the State tells us to do—including
> killing hundreds of millions of human beings and
> possibly destroying the earth. . . . Yet, Christians are
> called to *give* life rather than *take* it. . . . We cannot follow
> Christ today without losing something, without danger
> or sacrifice. . . . people find it more sane to contemplate
> nuclear suicide than civil disobedience. . . . we are held
> back by fear of consequences, but once the inner fear is
> conquered, the conseqences are quite bearable.

That December I reflected on this action in *Ridgeleaf*—
the Kirkridge newsletter.

> Where shall we look for the coming of Christ at
> Christmas? A TV reporter, commenting on the delight
> at the Pentagon with additional billions going to defense
> (offense?), said, "It's like Christmas at the Pentagon!" Is
> it now? In Salt Lake City, a group of church people,
> including Mormons, began a vigil in protest against the
> MX shell game planned for their state. Some of them do
> not believe it is God's will that their holy land should
> become so desecrated, only the will of the American
> Government. Shall we look for Christ wherever ordinary

people hold vigils, fly banners, hand out leaflets, and march for peace? The Christian Church is the only voluntary institution, located at every corner of city and town in America, which could mount a peace witness to say *No* to nuclear war and *Yes* to nuclear disarmament. If each of us makes peace witness where we live and work, we can become a leaven of hope. Could Christ come in you and me at Christmas?

Perhaps we could see Christ coming in the gray fortress-jail in Norristown, Pennsylvania. Christmas is crossing over. God crossed over to us in Christ, and every time we cross over to God's kingdom of peace, Christ comes again and Christmas happens. John Schuchardt, one of The Plowshares Eight and a lawyer, wrote from his prison cell:

If there is one word to describe our preparations for our action, our ten hours in the holding cells following arrest, our appearances in court, our lives in prison, it is JOY. This, too, describes the feeling of our communities and friends; each day brings new brightness: cards and letters filled with color, flowers, doves of peace, ocean waves, waterfalls, trees of life . . . Many of these greetings hang on our cell walls. We know that all of this is a gift; only God can bring joy and true happiness to a prison cell. The Old Testament prophets and Jesus point to strange paradoxes: joy in suffering, sacrifice, and resistance as the *only* alternatives to complicity in the crimes of the State. Spiritual death is the refusal to believe that peace is possible . . . Love leads us into the way of peacemaking even though we are full of fear, doubt and uncertainty. In this moment we somehow

crossed over. Cross over, too. Cross over now.
Brothers and sisters, we greet you all with love.

Christmas is crossing over from fear to love, from
serving the bomb to serving God. Whenever we cross
over, Christmas happens, Christ is born in us. Any
day can be Christmas Day, even today. Sisters and
brothers, let's cross over together.[3]

Perhaps the single most pervasive influence on us at
Kirkridge has been Daniel Berrigan. Dan has been
leading peacemaking retreats at Kirkridge for five years
now, often twice a year. Whether we title his event:
"Poetry and Politics," or "Prayer and Peacemaking," or
"Peacemaking as a Biblical Act," or "Picket and Pray,"
or whatever—Daniel always does the same thing . . .
Bible study. And what Bible study! Taking his
well-worn Bible, he reads a few verses, makes his
low-key, outrageous comments, followed by a period of
thirty minutes of quiet solitude, and then responses,
questions, sharing. His elfin humor, his wry grin . . .
Seeing him in New York, or at some action there or
elsewhere . . . the letters signed by a heart . . . Dan's
signature . . . Watching people come for these retreats,
and a few weeks or months later showing up with Daniel
at some action. Daniel—the pied piper of "divine
obedience" (read "civil disobedience") . . . for Christ.
Winning persons one by one—winning some of us a
little deeper each time. Spare, spartan, unintimidated
and unintimidating, except to those who would use
violence against other people. A fool for Christ.

Cindy and I were being quietly radicalized. The
exposure to peacemaking people was beginning to take.
Several Kirkridge Board members shared our growing

investment, and the entire Board was supportive of considering a serious fulltime peace ministry.

Kirkridge has a heritage hospitable to peace. John Oliver Nelson, founder of Kirkridge, has been a pacifist for decades, and a long time member of the Fellowship of Reconciliation—once serving as its president. Yet, he hadn't imposed this doctrine on Kirkridge either in terms of requirement for board members or its programming. And, in fact, there had been few peacemaking events over the years. But the heritage was hospitable, and the timing in the nation and the world was ripe.

In May 1981 the Kirkridge Board mandated a fulltime peace ministry, and authorized fund raising to support a full time peace minister.

The search for a peace minister kept turning up the name of Jo Clare Hartisig. A peace studies major at Colgate University, she was now in June 1981 graduating from Yale Divinity School, where she was president of her class. She had been organizing peacemaking on the YDS campus for three years. In April that year, she and several other YDS students witnessed against the "christening" of the attack submarine *USS Corpus Christi* at Groton, Connecticut. She was getting and giving her baptism by . . . water . . . hoping to help all of us avoid the baptism by fire. Jo Clare came to a Berrigan weekend that June, and the Spirit made things very clear to all concerned! Jo Clare joined us in September.

In the meantime, individuals, congregations, and denominations were beginning to respond to our appeals for partnership in peacemaking. Our intentions were to provide resources, energy, and leadership for those who wanted to develop peacemaking in their parishes. A group of a dozen congregations of many denominations in three states was formed. The Covenant Group has met several times a year to swap "peace stories," get ideas for liturgies inside and outside the walls, organize for legislative campaigns like the freeze, and generally encourage and pray for one another and for peace.

We also intended to connect with faculty and students in seminaries, seeking to provide resourcing for them in their efforts to penetrate the seminary scene with peacemaking energy and imagination. An annual retreat for seminarians has furthered these personal and institutional connections, and provided a little leaven for the seminary lump! Two comments from the peacemaking and seminary retreat in early 1983: "The weekend went beyond my expectations in the challenges it presented to my own personal life. I was pushed to the limit in the call to faith without fear"— "I expected a how-to event . . . write Congress, vote, pray, but instead, it challenged me to my Christian roots." Several of the participants in that retreat took part in a protest action at Groton later that winter. Our work with seminarians continues.

Jo Clare, working with Covenant Group pastors and laity, and others, helped organize and develop a church peacemaking witness in the Lehigh Valley. Easton, Bethlehem, and Allentown are the major cities of the Valley and the largest cities near Kirkridge. On Good Friday in 1982, a public Stations of the Cross march was held in Allentown—going from places like the Post Office (draft board and IRS issues) to the unemployment office, to a food bank, to an Hispanic neighborhood center, to a war memorial . . . to make visible the connections between giving enormous outlays of money to the Pentagon while taking huge resources away from services to the poor. Again on Good Friday in 1983, a Stations of the Cross was held, this time in Bethlehem.

The peace movement went public in America in 1982. The three chief visible expressions of its emergence were the Freeze Campaign, the June 12 march in New York, and the Pastoral of the Roman Catholic bishops. What joy to carry the Kirkridge banner on the streets of New York on June 12 and see so many friends! The huge European demonstrations in the late fall of 1981—the "peace conversions" of people like Billy Graham, the "repentance" of people like Hyman Rickover, McGeorge Bundy, and other former government leaders—the outspoken protest of Bishops Raymond Hunthausen in the State of Washington (including his widely publicized tax resistance) and Leroy Mattheisen in Amarillo, Texas—all were the visible ripples on a deep and rising tidal wave of protest against the arms race. It seemed that every month there was some new eruption of hope such as the gathering of thirty thousand women at the Greenham Common Air Base in Engand, in December of 1982—women who protested the planned emplacement of new U.S. missiles there in late 1983 by literally encircling the nine-mile-around base with their bodies, weaving yarn through its fencing. That summer, their American sisters established the Women's Peace Camp at the Army Depot in Seneca Falls, New York. As the deployment of Cruise and Pershing Missiles proceeded in the fall of 1983 and as tempers flared up at the inexcusable shooting down of Korean Air Lines Flight

007, the peace movement dug in its heels for patient witness in the dangerous Orwellian year of 1984.

Meanwhile, back at Kirkridge, our peacemaking sought to make more visible the connections between peacemaking and unemployment, peacemaking and the need to transform a badly flawed capitalist system, peacemaking and sanctuary for refugees from Central America, the homeless poor and arms race resisters.

Our hospitality ministry to peacemakers keeps on deepening. We are a place of sabbath for burnt-out peace people, a safe and open place for peace workers of diverse theology and practice to gather together. Jim Wallis describes such a gathering:

> We gathered at Kirkridge . . . Fifty-two leaders of the Christian peace movement met for more than two days of Bible study, prayer, fellowship and "discerning the times." Present were peace workers from nine denominational offices, members of religious communities, staff members from national peace and justice organizations, local organizers, pastors, theologians, and longtime peace activists.
>
> This was the first time that such a broad and diverse group had come together. . . .
>
> The gathering testified to the breadth and depth of Christian peacemaking in the U.S. churches. During the last session, people lifted up calls to resist Trident, to refuse war taxes, to stop the funding of MX, to join with Europeans to stop the Pershing II and Cruise Missiles, to further develop the abolitionist theme, to join together in congregation—and community-based witness, to deepen our roots in prayer, and much more. It was heartening to see that calls for both civil disobedience

and legislative initiatives against the arms race were felt to be complementary rather than competitive.

Throughout the time together voices testified to the connection between our labor for peace and our struggles for economic and racial justice. Many of those present had their roots firmly in the struggles of the poor and the oppressed. No longer can we allow the work of peace and the struggle for justice to be divided by those with vested interests or narrow visions. The Bible makes the spiritual and political linkage between the two absolutely clear.[4]

Peggy Scherer writes about the same retreat: "We came together for a retreat, rather than a planning session, because we believe that the threat posed by nuclear war is of such magnitude that our efforts for peace must be based first in prayer." Quoting the Catholic Bishops' Pastoral—"Peace is a gift from God"—she also quoted a woman at the retreat who said, "We need to learn how to be instruments of peace, rather than promoters of peace." She spoke of the many efforts "which [have] opened many eyes" and "the need of conversion . . . not only of those who threaten the world's future by stockpiling arms, but of ourselves and of the Church."[5]

It *is* like a conversion; the eyes of our hearts *are being skinned* in answer to our own prayers, and perhaps the prayer of Paul who keeps praying for "the eyes of your hearts [to be] enlightened, that you may know what is the hope to which he has called you" (Eph. 1:18)—the hope that waits at the heart of despair.

4
Hope-Work

In his book *Schindler's List* Thomas Keneally tells the story of a German industrialist, Oskar Schindler, who responded to the "Jewish question" by building from his own resources a concentration camp-factory in Cracow, Poland. Within its confines he sheltered thousands of Jews, finally transferring them to another safe haven in Czechoslovakia (Brinnlitz), as a besieged Reich consigned sixty thousand souls a day to the ovens of Auschwitz in a last mad attempt to effect the "Final Solution." A place on Schindler's list meant the hope of a future to an imprisoned Jew.

As the final weeks of the war wound down, prisoners at Brinnlitz began to feel safe inside Schindler's factory. The SS was not allowed to go inside the factory without Oskar. His presence somehow protected the Jews.

Oskar, however, was away on the day when an inspector from Gross-Rosen arrived and walked through the workshop with Untersturmführer Josef Liepold, the new Commandant.

The Inspector's orders . . . were that the Gross-Rosen subcamps (of which Brinnlitz was one) should be scoured for children to be used in Dr. Josef Mengele's medical experiments in Auschwitz. Olek Rosner and his small cousin Richard Horowitz, who'd believed they had no need of a hiding place here, were spotted racing around the annex, chasing each other upstairs, playing among the abandoned spinning machines. So was the son of Dr. Leon Gross . . . Further on in the inspection Roman Gintner's nine-year-old was discovered . . . [and] sent . . . to the gate with the other children. Frances Spira's boy, ten and a half years old, but tall and on the books as fourteen, was working on top of a long ladder that day, polishing the high windows. He survived the raid. The orders required the rounding up of the children's parents as well, perhaps because this would obviate the risk of parents beginning demented revolutions on the subcamp premises. Therefore Rosner, the violinist, Horowitz, and Roman Ginter were arrested. Dr. Leon Gross rushed down from the clinic to negotiate with the SS. He was flushed. The effort was to show this inspector from Gross-Rosen that he was dealing with a really responsible sort of prisoner, a friend of the system. The effort counted for nothing. [The party of fathers and sons traveled by train with armed escort to Auschwitz. On the way, the young] Olek turned his head against [his father] Henry's arm and began to weep. He would not at first tell Rosner what was wrong [but finally said he was sorry to drag his father off to Auschwitz], "to die just because of me." [His father] could have tried to soothe him by telling lies, but it wouldn't have worked. All the children knew about the gas.[1]

Today, all the children know about the bomb. And all the fathers and mothers know. Many parents yearn towards their children, wishing to protect them from a nuclear catastrophe, but know they cannot. Parents cannot surely prevent their children from being scoured out of their play and swept away in some mushroom cloud. Children also have their fears. Junior high school students responding to a survey in *Read* magazine listed the death of a parent and nuclear war as the two chief fears of tragedies that could overtake them, tragedies which they were powerless to control.[2]

There are moments when I believe that my children are on the train with me riding, towards a nuclear Auschwitz. What dark, foreboding sorrow not to be able to protect your children from being conscripted for holocaust. We simply can't stand to imagine our children's fiery deaths or slow radiation agonies without us, or perhaps any human beings nearby to aid them in their pain and terror. So we flip the TV knob, have another drink, work longer hours, or play more golf—whatever it is we do to banish such painful thoughts from our consciousness, and in doing so, we try to avoid *feeling* our despair. Robert Lifton, Yale psychologist, terms this exercise and its effects "psychic numbing."

Polls of recent years consistently find that two-thirds of the people of our country fear that there will be a nuclear war in their lifetime, and that they will not survive it.[3] Lifton writes:

> Undermined now is the fundamental parental responsibility, that of "family security." In the face of the threat of nuclear extinction, parents . . . doubt their ability to see their child safely into some form of functional adulthood. And the child must also sense . . . not only those parental doubts but the general inability of the adult world to guarantee the safety of children. In fact, there is growing evidence of a significant impairment to the overall parent-child bond, to the delicate balance between protection and love on the one hand, and the inner acceptance of authority on the other.[4]

I have mentioned my own difficulty in talking with my children about these things. I feel it to be a kind of intrusion upon their pursuit of happiness—a sort of discourtesy to question their future. I sense in them ambivalence: both hungering for honesty and a chance to acknowledge their own moments of despair, and perhaps a feeling that "Dad exaggerates these things," "he's into peace, and it's his thing," or even "look, leave me alone, let me enjoy even a few years of ignorant bliss, if that's what it really is."

Joanna Marcy has developed a theory and practice of what she calls "despair-work." Believing it is critical for our survival as a species, she invites us to allow ourselves to *feel* our despair about nuclear peril, and provides a process of working through our despair to an empowerment that enables us to face it, cope with it, and make creative use of its energy to do what we can to stop the arms race. Her purpose is to turn apathy and psychic numbing into experienced pain from which the promise of action arises. She points out that in our culture—to acknowledge despair goes against the compulsion of positive thinking. Despair is resisted because it represents a loss of control and an admission of powerlessness, traits that are virtually un-American. This is a despair different from the fear of our own death in the nature of things . . . a natural and good phenomenon. Societal extinction is unnatural, an evil, and unimaginably sad in the severing of the biological connections of the generations. She says that until we can grieve for our planet, our power of creative response to planetary crisis will be crippled. She writes:

Sometimes the blocked emotions of despair become accessible through dreams. The most vivid in my experience occurred after a dull job of perusing statistics on nuclear pollution. Before going to bed I had leafed through baby pictures of our three children to find a snapshot for my daughter's high school yearbook. In my dreams I behold the three of them as they appeared in the old photos, and am struck most by the sweet wholesomeness of their flesh. My husband and I are journeying with them across an unfamiliar landscape. The land is becoming dreary, treeless and strewed with rocks; Peggy, the youngest, can barely clamber over the boulders in the path. Just as the going is getting very difficult, even frightening, I suddenly realise that, by some thoughtless but unalterable prearrangement, their father and I must leave them. I can see the grimness of the way that lies ahead for them, bleak and craggy as the red moonscape and with a flesh-burning sickness in the air. I am maddened with sorrow that my children must face this without me. I kiss them each and tell them we will meet again, but I know no place to name where we will meet. Perhaps another planet, I say. Innocent of terror, they try to reassure me, ready to be off. Removed and from a height in the sky, I watch them go . . . three small, solitary figures trudging across that angry wasteland, holding each other by the hand and not stopping to look back. In spite of the widening distance, I see with a surrealist's precision the ulcerating of their flesh. I see how the skin bubbles and curls back to expose raw tissue, as they doggedly go forward, the boys helping their little sister across the rocks. I woke up, brushed my teeth, showered, had an early breakfast meeting, took notes for a research proposal. Still the dream did not let me go. As I roused Peggy for school, I sank beside her bed. "Hold me," I said. "I had a bad dream." With my face in her warm nightie, inhaling her fragrance, I found myself sobbing. I sobbed against her body, against her 17-year old womb, as the knowledge of all that assails it surfaced in me. Statistical studies of the effects of ionizing radiation, columns of figures on cancers and genetic damage, their import beyond utterance, turned now into tears, speechless wracking.[5]

But what came out of the wracking was a process that enables many of us to confess despair, finding in its deepest darkness a process through which Joanna recently led participants in a Kirkridge retreat on peacemaking.

Despair-work features: *Imaging:* allowing ourselves to imagine and acknowledge the affective energy in our fear and sorrow, releasing it to flow out with the energy of hope. *Waiting:* allowing the cocooning-time for our despair to incubate our pain into action. *Community:* Despair-work is not a solo venture. Our acknowledged pain makes visible our interconnectedness with one another, breaking taboos against despair, permitting it to be openly expressed in imagery, ritual, tears, rage, and plain talk—releasing blocked energy. "Through our despair, something more profound and pervasive than our despair comes to light. It is our interconnectedness, our inter-existence."[6] At the bottom of the pain, there is promise; at the bottom of despair, there is empowerment.

In that same retreat on peacemaking, Walter Wink opened the word of Ezekiel 37 to become flesh in us. We lay down on the floor, and allowed ourselves to imagine the dry bones of which Ezekiel writes. "What is the desert like? What kind of dryness? What do the bones

look, feel, taste, smell like? Is anyone else here?"
Someone then read Ezekiel's passage where the Spirit
of the Lord breathes upon these slain that they may live.
Flesh begins to grow again on the bones and the bones
are reconnected to one another—as in the gospel
spiritual (ankle bone to the leg bone, leg bone to the
thigh bone, etc.). Flesh keeps regathering around all the
bones until the congregation stands upon its feet—a
huge, lively living throng! It is a glorious death/resur-
rection image.

Walter invited us to imagine our skin—that precious
connector of creatures. We were invited to touch our
cheek, arm, leg . . . and then to imagine our skin flaying
off, being peeled off by fiery waves, until we were
literally without skin or any flesh—dry bones. We then
imagined again the reverse process of restoration. We
were trying to experience together the defleshing of
death by nuclear fire, and the enfleshment together—in
community by resurrection. After the exercise we
needed very much to reach out and touch one another,
to stand up together—a lively and living people!

I will never again be able to meditate on Ezekiel 37
without remembering that dismemberment and re-
memberment.

In another retreat group we explored Mark 5, the
story where the demoniac, the man with the unclean
spirit, asks that the evil spirits in him—legion in name
and number—might be taken out of him and put into
the herd of swine. This man lived among the tombs, and
was observed day and night, bruising himself with
stones and crying out and groaning. So we allowed
ourselves to fantasize ourselves as that man, wandering
among the tombs—those monuments of death in our

nuclear night—and groaning . . . how we groaned . . . how the groaning of many voices rose and fell and rose higher and the sound moaned on and on until, as though in response to some hidden baton, the groaning rose in a mighty crescendo to become a roaring shout of protest! It was as though "the whole creation has been groaning in travail together until now; and not only the creation, but we ourselves, who have the first fruits of the Spirit, groan inwardly as we wait for adoption as sons, the redemption of our bodies. For in this hope we were saved" (Rom. 8:22-24).

The groaning became a shout of hope, releasing enormous hoping energy. Today the whole creation is groaning—from toxic soaked earth to polluted rivers and skies, to the nightmares of children and parents, to the screams of the tortured in this era of widespread human torture. The groaning is getting louder. All of us are beginning to hear it. Surely God hears. Surely God is in our deepest groaning, working and praying for us that it might be a travail of giving birth to a new, liberated, and redeemed world order (Rom. 8:18-25). The creation may be pregnant with the children (Child) of God—whether to be stillborn, aborted, or borne in tears of joy—we do not know. But we are midwives, all of us attending the birthing of others and of ourselves. But the groaning is the thing! The groaning is our way into the darkness of our despair where we may in grace find the light of hope and stand up a lively, living throng of people who resist the destruction of creation and insist on its healing. One such groaning protest has come from the mind and heart of George Kennan, who writes:

This civilization we are talking about is not the property of our generation alone. We are not the proprietors of it; we are only the custodians. It is something infinitely greater and more important than we are. It is the whole; we are only a part. It is not our achievement; it is the achievement of others. We did not create it. We inherited it. It was bestowed upon us, and it was bestowed upon us with the implicit obligation to cherish it, to preserve it, to develop it, to pass it on—let us hope improved, but in any case intact—to the others who were supposed to come after us . . . I cannot help it. I hope I am not being unjust or uncharitable. But to me, in the light of these considerations, the readiness to use nuclear weapons against other human beings—against people whom we do not know, whom we have never seen, and whose guilt or innocence it is not for us to establish—and, in doing so, to place in jeopardy the natural structure upon which all civilization rests, as though the safety and the perceived interests of our own generation were more important than everything that has ever taken place or could take place in civilization: this is nothing less than a presumption, a blasphemy, an indignity—an indignity of monstrous dimension—offered to God![7]

Hope-work is borne out of despair-work. Doxology arises out of groaning. There has been an enormous yeasting of hope in this country and Western Europe in the last few years. Theologian Dorothee Soelle enables us to discern hope-work as liberation theology and as resistance theology. A theology of liberation puts its hope in mass movements, transformation of the current social and political scene, such as the movement Gandhi and his followers pursued in India, and the movement led by Martin Luther King, Jr., in this country. A theology of liberation was operating in the movement to abolish slavery in America one hundred and fifty years ago. A theology of liberation is operating in the national freeze movement today: the hope of changing current policy and transforming the nation. The "new" abolitionists, at one level, are hoping eventually to abolish war. A theology of liberation offers a persistent yes to the possibility of Christ the Liberator transforming culture. Liberators live by the ethical imperative of the gospel.

On the other hand, a theology of resistance puts little hope in mass movements, and offers a radical no to the evils of particular social systems, whether capitalism in our own country or a socialist utopia elsewhere. We may hope for change in the way things are, but do not expect such change. The gospel vocation is understood as digging in our heels in the face of injustice. In a darkening time when we cannot change things, we can refuse to be changed by things. We can refuse to be swept or seduced away from our own anchorage. If we cannot reverse the arms race, we can resist it patiently and passionately. If we cannot overcome, we can refuse to be overcome. If we cannot transform, we can refuse to be conformed. We can resurrect gospel terms like *endurance* and *withstanding* and *martyr*.

A theology of resistance is operative today in such actions as that taken by the Plowshares Eight. More than four thousand Americans were arrested in 1982 for nonviolent civil disobedience, and the number will be larger in 1983. Resistance actions are happening all across the country wherever there are nuclear weapons facilities, production, or storage—not just at the

Pentagon, Livermore Laboratories in California, the White House, etc. Tax resistance is growing. Resisters base their vocation in the spirit of Christ, the confronter of culture. They do not seek or make coalitions, they do not "ground their hope in the objective maturity of a given situation."[8] Resisters live by the eschatological imperative of the gospel.

Soelle says, "We need each other, liberationists and resisters." She encourages each of us to locate where we are on the liberation/resistance spectrum, and includes us all by citing a message on a Latin American poster: "Evangelico es luccha," the Gospel is the struggle.[9]

Hope-work changes colors like a chameleon, sometimes looking like liberation and other times looking like resistance. The Spirit of Christ knows no such distinctions, and we (while being helped by them) should not be fettered by them. Every hoping initiative is needed, from one end of the spectrum to the other, and each gospel initiative participates in the struggle. None of us knows when or whether a seed of courage will sprout out of dark ground, nor when a leaven of truth will permeate the lump of falsehood. We do know we are called to keep scattering seeds and sneaking in the leaven. What do we affirm in this culture and who are our fellow-liberaters? What do we resist in this culture and who are our fellow-resisters? What boundaries will we refuse to cross? What evils will break our silence?

An anguished appeal comes to Christians from Albert Camus:

What the world expects of Christians is that Christians should speak out, loud and clear, and that they should voice their condemnation in such a way that never a doubt, never the slightest doubt, could rise in the simplest [person]. That they should get away from abstraction and confront the blood-stained face history has taken on today. The grouping we need is a grouping of [people] resolved to speak out clearly and pay up personally . . .Perhaps we cannot prevent this world from being a world in which children are tortured. But we can reduce the number of tortured children. And if you don't help us, who else in the world can help us do this?

It may be, I am well aware, that Christianity will answer negatively. Oh, not by your mouths, I am convinced. But it may be, and this is even more probable, that Christianity will insist on maintaining a compromise or else giving its condemnations the obscure form of the encyclical. Possibly it will insist on losing once and for all the virtue of revolt and indignation that belonged to it long ago. In that case Christians will live and Christianity will die. In that case, the others will in fact pay the sacrifice. In any case, such a future is not within my province to decide, despite all the hope and anguish it awakens in me. I can speak only of what I know. And what I know which sometimes created a deep longing in me—is that if Christians made up their mind to it, millions of voices—millions I say—throughout the world would be added to the appeal of a handful of isolated individuals who, without any sort of affiliation, today intercede almost everywhere and ceaselessly for children and for [humanity].[10]

Nearly a million voices and faces were raised in hopeful protest on June 12, 1982, in the New York march. One of those voices belonged to Thomas Brinson, who served as a lieutenant in the Vietnam war.

He was carrying a banner on behalf of the fifty members of the Albany area chapter of the Vietnam Veterans of America. The blue and gold banner was billowing overhead. "We experienced the horror of war, and we don't feel it's justified for any means. It's not just our country. It's all the major countries of the world. It's the Soviet Union, it's France, it's China." Brinson said that he and his wife, Sarah, were marching not so much for themselves as for their two-year-old child and for the future of the world.[11]

Paul lives in Pennsylvania. Armed Services recruiters visited his high school, presenting Service educational opportunities and telling the golden story of $27,500 worth of four-year college support for students who sign up for one of the Services. (How galling that our tax money should be used to subsidize the seduction of our children into the military system as a way of saving money on college costs.) One of the gimmicks of the recruiters was to give students a sheet of paper in the style and shape of a bumper sticker. If a student sent in his name and his preferred department of service to the proper place, the sticker came back in two weeks reading, for example: "John Jones, United States Navy." Paul counted up the spaces on the sticker, sent in his information, and sure enough—two weeks later, his sticker came back reading: "You'll Never Get Me In"!

Marion Kimes is a wayfarer, a poet, and a friend. She spent some time near Seattle, participating in the work of the Pacific Life Community doing various kinds of witness at Ground Zero near the Puget Sound Submarine Base. Marion wrote us one time: "Last Wednesday we heard a worker from the base who quit work in March talk about her various motivations, and about the leafletting and what it meant to her, and what she feels it means to others 'inside.' She said, 'Here is this unmentionable subject, and here are these people who keep mentioning it every Thursday morning!' "

It used to be sex or death we couldn't mention. Now it's the nuclear peril and the insanity of governments, including our own, that is unmentionable in polite company. Mentioning the unmentionable is a form of gossiping the gospel, as they used to call it in the East Harlem Protestant Parish. Gossiping the gospel at home, at work, at play, at church. This is just a start. I want to suggest three additional, specific ways of doing hope-work. The first is naming the demons.

Naming the demons means using true names and refusing to use false names. The early Christians insisted on using the name of Jesus, and refused to stop preaching the resurrection in his name even when they were jailed for it (Acts 4).

Wherever evil lodges and breathes, there is the strategy of using false names in an effort to hide monstrosity and normalize the practice of horror. Auschwitz "was a phenomenon. The moral universe had not so much decayed there. It had been inverted, like some black hole, under the pressure of all the earth's malice—a place where tribes and histories were sucked in and vaporized, and language flew inside out. The underground chambers were named 'disinfection cellars,' the above ground chambers 'bathhouses.' "[12]

In George Orwell's *1984,* the Ministry of Truth was in charge of official lying. Its headquarters displayed the party slogans:

War Is Peace
Freedom Is Slavery
Ignorance Is Strength

Today the destabilizing MX Missile is named The Peacekeeper. Language is flying inside out again.

It is tempting to waste a lot of angry energy protesting such obscene and clumsy attempts to use false names and normalize plans for fast-strike atrocity. Humor helps. Satire saves. Thank God for people like Art Buchwald and Russell Baker!

Buchwald writes,

> You can say what you want about our military planners, but when it comes to naming mega-death weapons, they know their business. Digby Trident, who is in charge of market research at Defense, told me: . . . "The more innocent the name, the better chance we have of the public accepting it. Let's take the 'Cruise Missile.' The name was selected over others after a great deal of market research in on-the-street interviews. The pollsters asked people first how they felt about a new, improved 'Hiroshima Plus Missile' and received an overwhelmingly negative reaction. Then they were questioned how they'd like one called 'Sudden Death.' The male respondents said the name appealed to them because it reminded them of professional football. But most females said the first thing that came to their minds was a lot of families being wasted. Finally we asked what came to mind when they saw the words 'Cruise Missile.' The majority of those questioned said it made them think of a nice boat on a smooth sea. Eighty percent said they would buy a ticket on a Cruise Missile even if they didn't know where it was going."[15]

Russell Baker imagines a group of missiles talking over
The Peacekeeper and all the new language:

> "In the new world we have entered, doves are hawks and
> hawks are doves. You will soar proudly with the hawk
> emblazoned on your peacehead."
> "You're taking away our warheads?"
> "With a simple flick of the tongue we turn them into
> peaceheads."
> "How do we commit the fratricide?"
> "You don't commit it. It is too heinous a crime for
> American missiles. Fratricide means brother killing
> brother. By soaring deep under the Wyoming earth, you
> will tempt Soviet brother missiles to attack Wyoming . . .
> Imagine three Russian brothers, say, Ivan, Dmitri and
> Alyosha Karamazov . . . They roar in, one after the
> other, to disturb The Peacekeeper. Ivan hits first. Boom!
> What a mess! Radiation, foul gas, fire everywhere, just as
> Dmitri and Alyosha descend. What happens? The mess
> blows up Dmitri and Alyosha before they hit Wyoming,
> leaving Peacekeeper safe in the earth. That's fratricide."
> "But suppose a father missile comes along with them.
> What if the mess blows him up too?"
> "In that case, my dear Peacekeeper, we should have
> patricide . . . And what's more, if the brother and father
> missiles had brought along mattresses, planning to sleep
> that night in Wyoming, we could even have matricide . . .
> That's not all . . . If one of the missiles brought along a
> son and the mess on the ground caught him up in the sky,
> we would have sonsicide up."[14]

Naming the demons means using true names and
refusing to use false ones. It means calling a defense
industry a war machine, and a nuclear bomb a false
god—which leads us to a second mode of doing
hope-work: confronting idols.

Confronting idols has to do with idolatry and blasphemy. Co-opting the name of Christ (Corpus Christi) for an attack submarine *had* to be protested and was. "Not in His Name or Ours" was the slogan of the partially successful campaign to change the name of that engine of death.

Leviticus 19:4 reads, "Do not turn to idols, and cast no gods of metal. I am Yahweh your God" (JB). Our justificatory language for the conception, production, deployment, and use of nuclear weapons is theological. We say these weapons will save us, they are our final security, and in them we will and do trust. Today faith either dwells around the bomb or not at all. In first-century Rome, faith had to do with offering a pinch of salt before the bust of Caesar or refusing to offer it, for which the penalty was being torn to pieces by lions in the Coliseum. Today faith has to do with acquiescing in or protesting nuclear weapons as false salvation "objects of non-art" (Dan Berrigan's phrase).

The Bomb as God for security. The Bomb is God. The Bomb and God for security. God is the Bomb. The Bomb will save us. It's all theology; it's all bad theology—unbiblical, unchristian theology.

Some resisters throw blood, usually their own, on nuclear weapons or weapons facilities to require us "to confront the blood-stained face history has taken on today" (Berrigan) and to confront the idolatry involved. Maps of nuclear America are on bulletin boards in some churches, union halls, peace centers all across the country, to show people in Detroit and Lakeland, Amarillo and Atlanta, where the nearest death factories are to them. Many of the German people during World War II may not have known of the existence of the death camps until late in the war. But today it is public knowledge where the death factories are where Armageddon is being prepared. If there should be some kind of after-death beyond nuclear holocaust, we could not claim we didn't know.

Paul and his friends were run out of Ephesus just for saying that the little silver statues of Artemis, which had become popular and profitable, were no gods, but that Jesus was the embodiment of God (Acts 19). Those statues had become the economic staple of the town. We almost can hear them saying, "Think how many jobs are tied up in the silver statue industry!" Confronting idols has a long and honorable biblical history, a tradition being recovered in our time by those who refuse to bow down to the gods of metal because Yahweh is our God.

Confronting idols leads us to a third way of doing hope-work: *making connections visible.*

It was hope-work to point out that at the very time the Reagan administration was urging reduction of nutrition in the lunches of poor children, the White House was installing $209,000 worth of new chinaware—wags referred to it as Nancy Reagan's New China policy. Feasting at the White House/fasting for poor children—making connections visible.

"The Living Section" of the Wednesday, 1 December 1982 edition of the New York *Times* featured its lead article in old English type, "Food Gifts for Your Christmas," with sumptuous drawings and pictures of salmon platter Balducci's, ceramic casserole Dean El Delca, Mince Pie Rosemary Miller, Lebanese Sweets Le Baklava, and oodles more delicious and tempting gourmet delights—while visible in the left column of the page was a second article with the title: "Should U. S. Cut Funds for Child Nutrition?"[15]

Making connections visible between tax breaks for the rich and reduction of programs for the poor, bloating of the Pentagon budget and slashing of services for the old, sick, minorities, poor—Leonard Silk, an economist, quotes data demonstrating that military dollars create fewer jobs than other types of expenditure. One billion spent on the Department of Defense creates 48,000 jobs.

> However, an extra $1 billion would create 76,000 jobs if spent on sewer construction, 76,000 jobs if spent on public housing, 77,000 jobs if spent on nurses, 100,000 jobs if spent on teachers and 151,000 jobs if spent on the Job Corps. . . .

Professor Robert C. Sahr of Purdue University concludes that "nearly every other kind of Federal Government spending creates more jobs per billion dollars than does military spending." Further, most conservative and liberal economists are agreed that military spending tends to be more inflationary than civilian spending, especially because of the bottleneck problem of scarce engineering and other specialized skills and because military procurement is concentrated in a few industries, such as electronics and computers, which already enjoy strong demand. There is also concern that excessive military spending hurts national productivity growth compared with a country like Japan, which focuses its best talents on civilian programs. The most fundamental criticism of an excessively rapid military buildup is that it distorts the use of national resources, overstrains the budget, helps keep interest rates high, drags other investment and thereby weakens growth and employment.[16]

The connection between more money to the Pentagon and danger to public health was made by Anthony Lewis, *New York Times* columnist. Referring to an article by Dr. Howard H. Hiatt, dean of the Harvard School of Public Health, in *The New England Journal of Medicine,* Lewis notes that "the Reagan administration's plan to spend $1.6 trillion on defense in the next five years requires a massive reallocation of resources, [reducing funding for health]. Immunization programs . . . may save in treatment of disease as much as 10 times what they cost. But cuts in Federal Funds for 1982 will reduce the number of American children who can be immunized from 6.3 to 4.2 million. . . . Then there is research. The research budget of the Defense Department has been increased 26 percent . . . while that of the National Center of Health Services Research has been cut 45 percent. The cuts in fundamental biological and health research . . . 'will adversely affect the health of our own generation and of future generations.'[17] Lewis also mentions nutrition programs, which have been severely cut—$1.46 billion slashed from federal child nutrition programs, for one. The medical damage resulting from malnutrition or disease in early childhood may never be repaired and may be immensely expensive to society. 'Americans . . . might reasonably compare the 'savings' on such health programs with the $4.5 billion allocated this year for the MX program; the $100 million cost for each of the 100 projected B-1 bombers . . . and the $4.2 billion requested over the next seven years for civil defense.'[18]

By the time this book is published, one or more of the above programs may have been scrapped, altered, increased . . . whatever. The point, of course, is that there continue to be competing claims for our dollars, talents, energies, and investments—and the more that goes to the military for preparation of death, the less will be available for human services preserving life.

Hope-work involves committing ourselves to a few, specific, particular people and being willing to risk our own lives on their behalf. It isn't the big picture for most of us, but many millions of little picture which, when put together, make up a vast and living collage of human groaning and hoping.

Thomas Merton wrote a young activist friend:

> Do not depend on the hope of results. When you are doing the sort of work you have taken on, essentially an apostolic work, you may have to face the fact that your work will be apparently worthless and even achieve no result at all, if not perhaps results opposite to what you expect. As you get used to this idea, you start more and more to concentrate not on the results, but on the value, the truth of the work itself. And there, too, a great deal has to be gone through, as gradually you struggle less and less for an idea and more for specific people. The range tends to narrow down, but it gets much more real. In the end, it is the reality of personal relationships that saves everything. . . . the big results are not in your hands or mine, but they suddenly happen, and we can share in them; but there is no point in building our lives on this personal satisfaction, which may be denied us and which after all is not that important.[19]

Oskar Schindler committed himself to a few thousand Jews who came his way in the Nazi deathcamp hysteria of Poland in the early 1940s. Justice Moshe Bejski, Supreme Court of Israel, says of him: "According to a Talmudic saying, He who saves one soul, it is as if he saved the entire world. Oskar Schindler saved many and he is among those who saved the honor of mankind."[20]

Hope-work finally requires us to face our enemies.

5
Facing Our Enemies

A Bible study group was discussing the text "Love your enemies." We were asking, "Who is the person toward whom you feel most hostility?" All at once a woman breathed hard and said "It's my husband!" It took her by surprise, as it did her husband, another group member. It reminded all of us that much of the anger we harbor, and the actual verbal and even physical violence we experience—both as givers and receivers—takes place in the family. Loving "enemies" has to begin at home.

As a child I was raised not to express my anger in a public or upsetting way. Anger was to be contained in the interest of decorum—surface harmony at the cost of emotional honesty. I wasn't even aware of the considerable anger building up in me at my father, my wife, the church, myself, until my middle age.[1] In my own family, my daughter Barbara and I had trouble communicating with each other, even though there was a deep layer of belonging and real, if sometimes awkwardly expressed, affection.

At one period, Barbara was going to college part time, working full time, and doing well. I was providing tuition support. One night we were talking on the phone when she brought up her desire to buy a car—a Mustang, which at that time was selling for five or six thousand dollars. I wasn't in favor of the proposed purchase, to understate the matter. Before I could stop myself, I heard myself saying, "Here I am supporting you; you're just making it; how can you possibly make car payments without going into debt?" She said it was her own business, and all of a sudden, there we were arguing in our old, destructive behavior pattern. After a couple minutes of it, she burst into tears and hung up.

She was in Columbus, Ohio, and I was five hundred miles away, in Pennsylvania. I didn't sleep well that night. The next morning I wrote her a letter affirming her right to buy a car if she could swing it without derailing her college work, and assuring her of my continuing support for her tuition, regardless of what she decided to do, and telling her I loved her. A week went by. Two weeks. No word from Barbara. I waited. Three weeks were gone. Part of me wanted to rush to the phone, call her, and say, "Honey, how are you? I love you." And another part of me insisted on waiting. I wanted to respect her enough to let her respond how and when and if she chose to do so. And I had to be willing to eat my anxiety and unrequited (for the moment) father's love.

After a month, a letter came from her. She wrote in part,

All my life I've needed your approval for everything. If I didn't get it I was lost. I only got it when I was doing what you thought I should be doing. I guess that's why our conversation on the phone went the way it did. I made a decision and you disapproved. What I'm trying to say is—I want to grow up, I want to be my own person. I want to make my own choices for myself and pay my own prices whether you or any one agrees with them. . . . I love you, Dad. . . .   Barbara.

Somewhere in those years she had started signing her letters "Barbara" instead of "Barbie." She had grown up, and was helping me to grow up along with her. I learned that I was a novice at loving enemies in my own family.

What about loving enemies in the neighborhood, community, or congregation?

Parker Palmer suggests biblical images of community in triptych form. On the left, the garden before the fall—archetypal, original creation, natural harmony. "They were naked and unashamed." Unafraid of intimacy. On the right, the shining city of Peace described in Revelation, "where every tear shall be wiped away and death shall be no more." The problem with both images, says Palmer, is that they are outside of history, one before it and the other after it. Literally out of this world. Each, therefore, is an unreal image of what real community will be like inside our history. He posits a definition: "Community is that place where the person you least want to live with always lives! Later I developed a corollary: 'And when that person moves away, someone else arises to take his or her place!' "[2]

Palmer suggests a third biblical image for the center of the triptych. It is the scene of The Last Supper. One is breaking bread, passing a cup, and saying, "Someone here will betray me." And another is asking, "Who is the greatest among us?" Palmer says *this* is what community is like, and adds that Jesus did not leave the table.

The discipline of "staying at the table" is the necessary *modus vivendi* for facing and loving our enemies at home, in the community, and among the nations. We are given to one another in the blood family. We are locked into a nuclear family with the Russians, from which there is no safe exit ever. We must stay at the table with them. For long periods of time we may be locked into relationships in the congregation, neighborhood, or city that we would never choose, but can't escape. Anger and hatred build up in such situations, in part because we can't get out of them.

I think of a man in one of the congregations I served who was a *bête noire* to me. He was a recognized leader and person of power and authority in the congregation. After he and I locked horns on some vital matters, I began to feel that he was out to get rid of me—we were in some fashion vying for control of that church. I dreamed about him often, and often the dreams were nightmares. He and I could never find our way to a reconciliation, only to an accommodation—a courteous truce. Only looking back years later, can I admit to myself that he was an enemy in my eyes, that I felt fear and anger towards him, and was sometimes paranoid about his alleged attempt to get rid of me. Why this man, why me? Once in a while I prayed for him, and sometimes when I meditated on his face, I felt a softening towards him. But I never acknowledged such feelings to him, nor did he reach out to me.

J. W. Stevenson's book *God in My Unbelief* is the story of a pastor in a church in Crainie, Scotland. John Forsyth was a thorn in his side and in the side of the Kirk Session.

> One night, at the end of a long altercation, two of the older men said they could not go on; they were broken by the quarrelling. I walked up and down the road afterwards, trying to think how peace was to be restored amongst us, praying that John Forsyth might be forgiven

for the hurt he was doing. As I turned in my walking, I came within sight of his window, and I stopped; thinking of the man sitting there behind the drawn blinds. Something cried out in me because I had not been able to mend what was broken—like the cry of the disciples, "Why could we not cast him out?" In the cry I knew what I had never known before. I had often been praying for him; but I knew in the flash of that moment, that, even in my prayer, I had been separated from him. I had been looking at his sin, and judging it, and asking that he might be forgiven. I had not been standing beside him, my sinfulness beside his sinfulness, asking that we might both be forgiven. Christ had been seeking me, too, in this; and I had not discerned Him. This was the Cross . . . His seeking, and my blindness and disobedience. This was the Cross . . . not far back in history, but happening now in Crainie, because of me and for me . . . As I stood there, watching that window, I knew that I had been brought there. What John Forsyth needed, I needed. I was entirely one with him in it. It was not something he needed more, or I needed less. I had suddenly understood the Cross as I had never understood it before. And the man whom God had chosen for me to stand beside for the opening of my eyes was the man who was destroying the work of my ministry by his opposition and driving sleep from me by his accusations. Something in me had required that it should be this particular man and no other.[3]

Is it possible that in the mystery of God's pain-filled providence, father and daughters, clergy and laity need each other to grow up; Arabs and Jews need each other to break through to a new humanity; Northern Irish Catholics and Protestants need each other; Hindus and Moslems need each other . . . and . . . Russians and

Americans need each other? If we find reconciliation seemingly impossible in the family or in the family of the church, how shall we hope for it in the family of nations? For one thing, it may be harder to love the one we have seen than to love the one we have not seen. For another, we begin to understand that, whatever small progress we may hope for between enemy nations, only grace, the transformation of converted hearts and minds, will move us to mutual repentance and forgiveness. We need and seek something deeper than military and political accommodation, both of which are absolutely essential to allow time and opportunity for deeper reconciliation. But when we talk about enemy nations refraining from mutual annihilation, we are not just talking about the most urgent task on the human agenda, but also about peace as a gift from God, the skinning of our eyes, the conversion of our hearts.

Governments get their people to be willing to wipe out an enemy nation or population by dehumanizing their enemies. Hitler persuaded the German people that the Jews were a threat to the purity of the Aryan race, and therefore were not only expendable, but had to be eliminated so that the German version of "true humanity" would flourish. It is worth noting today that those who went into the ovens of Auschwitz, along with the Jews, were blacks, Communists, and homosexuals. In our own version of Western culture in this country, when prejudice towards one of these groups arises, prejudice towards the others is not far behind. So today, the heightening anti-Communist fervor inspired by the current administration also stirs up anti–Semitism, the resurgence of the Klan and more respectable racism (as in the 1983 Chicago mayoral election), in addition to mounting attacks upon the human rights of gay and lesbian people.

Growing up American meant that as a youngster I saw movies with A-rabs (long A), who were usually dirty, scruffy stand-ins in some desert setting for the likes of Lawrence of Arabia or some other blond conqueror from Europe. I learned to have contempt for Arab peoples without ever meeting one.

I also learned about kikes, gooks, wops, slants, spades, etc. . . . And during World War II, I learned that Japanese people had enormous teeth—very scary teeth—teeth that glowered down at me from billboards of movies about the traitorous Japs. Think what the term *being japped* has come to mean in our country— (like the phrase, "he tried to Jew me down." Sometimes I like to say, "he tried to Christian me up!") How easy it was for us, in fear and enemy hatred, to intern thousands of people of Japanese origin during those years, disregarding their constitutional rights, without the slightest evidence of any danger to this country. Only recently has Congress acknowledged that injustice. My conditioning about Germans was so effective that to this day, when I hear a gutteral voice or the sound of a clicking heel, Nazi-fear rises out of my gorge. What delicious irony that Volkswagen, Mercedes-Benz, Datsun, Toyota, and Honda are omnipresent among us! How quickly we came to admire the Japanese for their efficient industries, even to asking them to do it here, à la the 1983 Toyota-GM business agreement in California. The West Germans are now our major allies in Europe. So, as perceived threats shift, and former enemies become allies, our enemies are face-lifted into friends. We endow enemy nations with evil qualities which we teach to our people and our children as conditioning for killing the enemy, if necessary, in some national, holy crusade.

Enemy thinking runs deep in every nation. Americans are probably no better and no worse than other peoples in that regard. Since World War II, the Soviet Communists have been America's favorite enemies. Indeed the enmity began with the revolution of 1917. Joe McCarthy and the House Un-American Activities Committee nourished on the rising tide of enemy thinking in the early fifties.

In March 1983, President Reagan, speaking to the National Association of Evangelicals in Orlando, Florida, said that belief in God should make Americans join him in opposing a nuclear freeze and pressing a vast buildup of U.S. weapons. There is sin and evil in the world, the President said, and we are enjoined by Scripture and the Lord Jesus to oppose it with all our might. He said Soviet Communism is the focus of evil in the modern world. That particular audience cheered as an orchestra played "Onward Christian Soldiers."[4] Scary, knee-bent theology to promote chauvinist politics. Scary and unbiblical. Offensive . . . literally. Makes one think of the blind fury of the Crusades or Reichstag rhetoric. Claiming that God is on our side is the oldest and by far the most dangerous form of nationalism. At least the Russians don't do that!

But what about the Russians? What could it possibly mean to love the Russian enemy, to face the Russian enemy?

Of course, we have principled differences with the Russians—important differences. We deplore their treatment of Jews and their own dissidents. We deplore the absence of civil liberties, the invasion and occupation of Afghanistan, the crushing of Poland, and the support of left-wing tyrants around the world. You and I would not want to live under such a system of government. (Though we can't be proud of the way we Americans have cozied up to and provided military support for right-wing dicatorships all over the world—South Korea, the Philippines, South Africa, Argentina, Chile, and throughout Central America. Some of our best friends have been or are the Shah, Somoza, Marcos, Argentina's military rulers who "disappeared" thousands of their own people, and countless Central American tyrants who kill and torture their own dissidents with U.S. weapons, while making their markets available to our multinational corporations. It turns out that what we love, in terms of our visible support, is not so much democracy as capitalism with an anti-Communist face. Anti-Communism has become a national god, in whose name any and every inhumanity is tolerable.)

There are three faulty assumptions in our thinking about the Russians.[5] First, the assumption that the Soviet government is the incarnation of evil in the world. Once we make that assumption, then *anything* we do or prepare to do to such an enemy is OK. We see where that kind of ideological, theological fundamentalism leads. In Israel, Prime Minister Menachem Begin asserts it is God's will for Israel to have the disputed West Bank and Gaza Strip, and despite treaties or other arguments, the ideology prevails. In Iran, Khomeini paints Americans as the focus of evil in the world. The corollary of this assumption is that the American government is the incarnation of good in the world. Not long ago Jim Wallis of *Sojourners* led a retreat for some fifty top military officers. He found it frightening that the motivation of many of them is profoundly religious. They believe they are doing God's will by preparing to obliterate the enemy.

Contrary to such theological fundamentalism and national idolatry is the gospel declaration that we have all sinned and fallen short of the glory of God, that all persons, institutions, and nations are sinful, including ourselves (Rom. 5). Biblical Christianity prohibits demonizing adversary nations and angelizing our own. American leaders are just as capable of making a first strike nuclear attack as Soviet leaders. So which nation is more dangerous? Both nations are very dangerous.

The second faulty assumption in our thinking about the Russians is that the Russian people are expendable. This is the line of thinking that says we are willing to eliminate Russian people, tens of millions of them, should it prove necessary to protect our national security. Since it is not possible for anyone to win a *second strike* nuclear war, it seems that we are preparing for a *first srike* nuclear war. That's crazy. There's no way to zap them without getting zapped by them and vice versa. Right now, you and I are paying for and thus implicitly supporting the planning, building, and deployment of weapons for the killing of millions of people. Schell writes:

> Therefore, when we hide from ourselves the immense preparations that we have made for our self-extermination, we do so for two compelling reasons. First, we don't want to recognize that at any moment our lives may be

taken away from us . . . and, second, we don't want to face the fact that we are potential mass killers. The moral cost of nuclear armament is that it makes of all of us underwriters of the slaughter of hundreds of millions of people and of the cancellation of future generations. . . . Strategy thus commits us all to actions that we cannot justify by any moral standard. . . . To be targeted from the cradle to the grave as a victim of indiscriminate mass murder, is degrading in one way, but, to target others for similar mass murder is degrading in another, and in a sense, worse way.[6]

In Christian terms, if we are called to die for Christ, are we also called to kill for Christ? Where in the New Testament does it say that we are called to kill for Christ?

In a January 1983 sermon, a Bethlehem, Pennsylvania pastor tried to locate such a vocation in the New Testament. He ascribed such a warrant to Paul who, he asserted, intended to separate love and justice—embody love in the church and embody justice in the state. He quoted Paul as saying that the state has the God-given right to be a terror . . . to execute [God's] wrath on the wrongdoer (Rom. 13:3,4). He continued, "If the church teaches that there are no moral grounds whatsoever which would legitimize the use of nuclear weapons, and that Christians ought not to participate in any way whatsoever in the manufacturing and use of such weapons, then I'm afraid that we will deny our government the right to a 'sword' powerful enough to bring 'terror' to those who would oppose human rights. We are all sad to be living in a day when the sword guaranteeing justice has to be represented by the awesome power of nuclear arms, but in such a world we live.''[7]

This preacher got a standing ovation from his congregation after the sermon. What can be said? It can be said that there is no biblical way to separate love and justice. It can be said that a population about to be bombed (if it could reflect on its impending obliteration) would not be interested in a theological distinction about a bombadier who is loving in his family or church, but who murders as a servant of the state. (Robert Lifton speaks of the Nazi doctors who worked during the day in Auschwitz and went home at night to their families as living in moral schizophrenia.) It can be said that America is as sinful a nation as Russia, that before God we all have sinned and fallen short. It can be said that the Spirit may even be teaching us new things beyond what earlier theologians articulated, including Paul. It can be said that there is no way to justify such state-killing from the lips or life of Jesus.

The third faulty assumption in our thinking about the Russians is that our nation has the right to exterminate another society. This is akin to the second assumption, but its essence is that our nation has the right of genocide in pursuit of national interest. Who has the right of genocide? Does Russia? Does America? Hitler thought he did, hence the holocaust. If we believe even a little bit in the gospel of Christ, we know that no nation, religion, or ideology has the right of genocide. Indeed, according to Jesus' picture of the last judgment in Matthew 25, the *nations* (not individuals alone, but nations) will be judged on the basis of their treatment of "the least of these"—the least able to protect themselves from danger or death, the little

ones, the poor, the powerless, the stranger, the enemy,
the defenseless civilian populations.

Theologically speaking, as Christians we believe that
Christ was at the point of ground zero in Hiroshima—
that the face of Christ looked out of each pair of eyes in
Auschwitz. The crucifixion of Jesus keeps on happening wherever human beings suffer. Schell comments on
the words of Jesus, " 'If thou bring thy gift to the altar,
and there rememberest that thy brother hath aught
against thee; Leave there thy gift before the altar, and
go thy way; first be reconciled to thy brother, and then
come and offer thy gift.' We who have planned out the
deaths of hundreds of millions of our brothers, plainly
have a great deal of work to do before we return to the
altar. Clearly, the corpse of mankind would be the least
acceptable of all conceivable offerings on the altar of
this God."[8]

The corpse of mankind would be the ultimate Corpus
Christi. This would apparently be acceptable to some
Christians and indeed, may be viewed as part of God's
plan. Hal Lindsay describes "The Rapture," the
superhope of true believers: "There is a time coming
. . . during this generation when . . . every true believer
in Jesus will disappear from the Earth. . . . all believers
will be changed from mortal to immortal . . . without
ever dying. . . . The incredible promise is that we will
not be here on Earth when the horrible events we see
shaping up before our eyes take place . . . (we'll be in
one of the many rooms in the Father's house). At the
end of the seven-year Tribulation, when man is at the
brink of annihilation in an all-out [nuclear] war, Jesus
the Messiah will personally return and stop it. And all of
us who believe now will return with Him in glorified

bodies. . . . This beginning period of the new world will last for 1,000 years. . . . It will only work when the Messiah runs it."[9]

It must trouble some of Lindsay's alleged millions of readers to learn that there is room for only 144,000 of them in the Father's house. Limited room in that inn. It must trouble others of us that such a view encourages people to do nothing about trying to reverse the arms race, both because only the Messiah himself could do it, and hopefully, they'll be part of the lucky lottery winners whisked away just in time. It is a despairing theology that asserts that God's will is that the world should end in annihilation. Richard Niebuhr espouses a different view: "We [Christians] are not those who are being saved out of a perishing world, but those who know the world is being saved."

What about the Americans?

We differ from the Russians and other European nations in that we have never suffered a modern war on our own soil. We have not yet had *our* cities bombed, *our* forests napalmed, *our* children murdered before our eyes—their screams ringing in our ears forever. Nor do we carry in our hearts the restraints that accompany remembrance of such things. In every major Russian city there are war memorials. And even today throughout Russia, devastating signs of World War II abide. We did not lose twenty million women, men, and children in that war. War has been for Americans a thing "over there," even when "there" was Vietnam and coming bloodily into our living rooms through our television sets.

George Kennan writes, "But we must remember that it has been we Americans who . . . have taken the lead in the development of this sort of . . . [nuclear] weaponry. It was we who first produced and tested such a device; we who were the first to raise its destructiveness to a new level with the hydrogen bomb; we who introduced the multiple warhead; we who have declined every proposal for the renunciation of the principle of 'first use,' and we alone, so help us God, who have used the weapon in anger against others, and against tens of thousands of non-combatants at that."[10] And who did it twice. We have broken the human barrier on the use of nuclear weapons. We have demonstrated that it is possible for human beings to do that to other human beings—for we have done it.

We are blessed with a political system in which we can protest what our government is doing or proposing. We can elect and dis-elect leaders. We can engage in civil disobedience knowing that we still will be given due process, that we will not be "disappeared" or put in a psychiatric hospital or sent to Siberia. Thank God we live under such a political system! But our responsibility is the greater! We do not simply represent ourselves, our own views and convictions. We have also to represent, speak on behalf of, protest to the world about those who live under political systems where they are denied such rights. In the matter of nuclear war—we have to speak out for the Russian people who do not want such a war, as well as for the American people. President Eisenhower once said, "The time will come when the people of the nations will insist so much on peace that their governments will have to give it to them." We are now in the time when such speaking out and living out must be done—and *we* must do it on behalf of Russians, and indeed, Third World countries who suffer from all governments' spending on weapons. Just because the people of Russia can't protest injustices to *their* rulers is no reason for us Americans to give up *our* civil liberties! But rather, more reason for us to insist on them for our own sake and the sake of the Russians as well.

In this context we are cursed with an economic system in which the profit motive fuels the arms race. Once again, it was President Eisenhower who was prophetic. In his farewell address as President, he warned us about the growing danger of the military-industrial complex. That was twenty-five years ago when that complex was in its infancy. Today it is a monster that is not just two-headed. In his book, *The Iron Triangle: The Politics of Defense Contracting,* Gordon Adams documents the links between huge defense contracting companies, Pentagon buyers, lobbyists, and executives, and the members of Congress who appropriate the money to pay for it all.[11] Eisenhower's two-headed monster now has three heads. There is a beltway moving between the Pentagon and other departments of government and the huge defense contracting companies: General Dynamics, General Electric, United Technologies, Bechtel, Boeing, etc. It is obscene to watch the top leadership personnel going to and fro across that beltway: the private payoff is enormous and corrupting; the cost to the nation's representative system is incalculable.

But we must add a fourth head to these three heads: Our taxes pay for the American universities where billions of dollars worth of Pentagon research is done.[12]

And we must add a fifth head: the PACs, those political action committees representing vested interest groups, many of which are reactionary and support the ingrown, embedded system that funds the militarist policies of our government. So we have a military-industrial-congressional-academic-vested interest complex! We have a five-headed monster, a pentagon-shaped juggernaut slouching its way across our country: robbing the poor, disinheriting the middle class, gorging the rich and the military, and plundering the treasure of this country's wealth, brains, and energy to imagine and create a whole world.

Once when driving north on Route #395 in Washington, D.C., I noticed the green highway sign detailing the next exit.

> Route 27
> Washington Blvd.
> Pentagon
> Arlington Cemetery
> *Exit Only*

A sign more revelatory than intended. Just as plain—a continuing arms race leads to *Exit Only* extinction.

This is the kind of thing Paul was thinking of when he wrote of "principalities and powers" and said that we are contending against more than flesh and blood (Eph. 6:12). It isn't that people who work for the Pentagon are bad people. We pay for what our representatives tell them to do. So, morally, we are on the same level as they. Rather, they, like the rest of us, are victims as well as agents of the militarist juggernaut. The actual and potential evil lodged in the system that creates, nourishes, and preserves a Pentagon or Kremlin is in our psyches as well as our systems. We are sinners. So we need more than legislative pluralities for a nuclear freeze, important as that is. We need to have the eyes of our hearts skinned. We need conversion. We need to face our enemies and stop defacing them. We must put a good face on our enemies so that we can love them. We need to feel the fear and terror and anguish of those who oppose us, both in other nations and within our own, and to have some sense of our kinship. For we all—Americans and Russians—are contending against more than flesh and blood, those principalities and powers that ratify killing and make mass murder honorable.

We make the enemy have an evil face.

Caspar Weinberger believes today that the threat of the Soviet Union is as great as Hitler's "so great that every consideration of domestic politics must be subordinated to it."[13]

Consider what such a belief means. It means that Weinberger sees the face of Hitler when he thinks as he does, all day, every day, about the Soviet threat. Americans came to believe during World War II that Hitler was as close to Evil incarnate as it was possible for human beings to get. There was Genghis Khan, Attila the Hun, and Hitler. So Weinberger comforts himself, and tries to persuade the rest of us, that no matter what evil we are preparing to do the Russians, it's entirely justified because they are close to the agents of Evil itself, "the focus of evil," etc.

The enemy either has an evil face, or no face at all. Sometimes we even deface our friends. Zbigniew Brzezinski gave an unintended look into his heart in an article he wrote on the hostage crisis in Iran.[14] He says the hostage families were about to come to Washington to be welcomed by the President and staff. Brzezinski decided not to meet them, deliberately not to see their faces, so that he would not suffer the vulnerability of being softened by human considerations, and possibly deterred from taking action later that might result in the death of some of the hostages, on behalf of national security. He protected himself against the possibility of being humanized, lest his will to make death-dealing decisions be compromised.

It is this detached, faceless inhumanity that may yet lead us to extinction. Our military leaders, and presumably those of Soviet Russia, engage in Think Tank War Games—a kind of deadly serious Atari. In such think tanks, the gamesmen are isolated and insulated in an abstract, bloodless, impersonal environment. They contemplate buttons that when punched result in the distant deaths of millions . . . dealing in "acceptable losses . . . collateral damage . . . city busting . . ." These euphemisms flesh out to the murder of tens of millions of individual human beings . . . such as you or me or our children.

At the 1982 Annual Meeting of the American Psychological Association, several papers were given on the psychology of warmaking.

Morton Deutsch of Columbia University suggests that nuclear weapons were "psychologically seductive," largely because they provide "a tremendous emotional kick for those with strong power drives." The kick comes, he said, because the stakes are high, decisions have to be made quickly, and use of the weapons is inherently aggressive. Dr. Deutsch also thinks the tidy, abstract character of nuclear war scenarios "appeal to the talented, imaginative, gamesmen" who are the leading strategic analysts in the United States and Soviet Union. Meanwhile, he lamented, "the real horrors of a nuclear war are not faced" and some way must be found to make them "psychologically real."[15]

At the same conference, "Roger Fisher, professor of law at Harvard University, [offered] a simple suggestion to make the stakes more real. He would put the codes needed to fire nuclear weapons in a little capsule, and implant the capsule next to the heart of a volunteer, who would carry a big butcher knife as he accompanied the President everywhere. If the President ever wanted to fire nuclear weapons, he would first have to kill, with his own hands, that human being. 'He has to look at someone and realize what death is—what innocent death is. It's reality brought home.' "[16]

To bring it all the way home, we might agree with the Soviets to follow the medieval practice of exchanging hostages from our "royal" families—in this case, members of the Reagan/Weinberger and Andropov/Gromyko families—as a deterrent to firing the first nuclear weapons. Fewer people might be running for President under such a policy.

We must find ways of *allowing our humanity to govern our behavior*. We must find ways of seeing our adversaries with their families, of allowing our family-hood with the Russians to come into our consciousness. We are talking about nothing less than the conversion of our hearts. Our vocation, then, is to put a human face on our enemies.

Occasionally something happens in the news that sneaks through our enemy-thinking defenses and skins the eyes of our hearts. In the fall of 1982, the first Amerasian children, with American GI fathers and Vietnamese mothers, were allowed to come to America. On the front page of the October 1, 1982, *New York Times* is a picture of six of these children—laughing, smiling, bright, vivacious—very attractive and appealing children. The children look different from their peers in Vietnam today. It is clear that their fathers were American soldiers during the war, which makes the lot of these children hard. On an inside page, is a photo of Gary Tanous of Vancouver, Washington, being reunited with his daughter, Jean Marie, in Ho Chi Minh City. She was one year old when he last saw her; now she is fifteen. "The touching, if anxious, reunion . . . was a big hug. 'At first she was very nervous, as I was . . . but she loosened up a lot and so have I. It will be fine.' "[17]

It happened that I was watching the evening news on TV at this time. All of a sudden, here were the Amerasian children, and here was Gary Tanous . . . smiling through his tears and saying, "These children aren't refugees, they're our children."[18] Of course! Of course, they *are* our children, and *also* refugees. And of course, the Russians *are* our brothers and sisters, and *also* our enemies.

But how shall we love the enemies running our country? All of us demonize, to some degree, those who see things differently. Among those I am tempted to demonize and deface is President Reagan. I resent him because I think he favors the rich, doesn't care about the poor, and exacerbates our relationship with the Russians instead of demonstrating statesmanship to improve U.S.—Soviet relations. How can I love this "enemy"—put a human face on Reagan?

Satire helps. You may remember that when the nuclear freeze movement began to get visibly successful, Reagan attempted to discredit it and those involved in it as being manipulated, controlled, and even funded by the Kremlin. (Not long after, the FBI disproved his allegation.) Sometime later, a small church in Idaho sent a letter to Russia marked on the outside with a huge KREMLIN. It read in part, "Dear Kremlin, our President has told us that you folks are funding the peace movement in our country. We are a small church out here in Idaho with limited resources. We have a tiny peace group started, and we would like to apply for a grant."

Prayer helps. It also helps me to see President Reagan and Andropov as victims, as well as agents, of nuclear evil. They, too, are caught up in the grip of the principalities and powers. They, too, are human beings. I can pray for each of them—and do. And when I am praying for them, if I am touched by grace like that pastor in Crainie, Scotland, I may be able to recognize that I am standing beside them, and we all need forgiveness. I, as much as they. We all might practice meditating on the face of an enemy.

We carry images in the eyes of our hearts, giving us hope and energizing our faith in dark times. One of these, for me, came when Anwar Sadat and Golda Meir were being interviewed during his peace mission in 1977 by Barbara Walters. The interview took place a couple of days after Sadat's trip from Cairo to Jerusalem. It happened that on the day he left Cairo, Sadat's first grandchild was born. There they sat—

opposing heads of state who recently had been ordering the killing of one another's children. Now they were joshing back and forth. Meir reminded Sadat of how he used to refer to her as "that mean old lady." In her lap she had a small package wrapped and tied with a bow.

At one point in the conversation, she looked at him and said, "I understand that your first grandchild was born the day you flew from Cairo." He nodded and smiled. She continued. "I have been a grandmother for many years. I have a gift for your grandchild." She leaned towards him, handing him the little package. As he reached over to receive it, his chin visibly trembled. So did mine, as I watched. In that moment, I felt that when we come to care enough about all the children and grandchildren, we will find ways to make peace and heal creation.

6
Keeping Creation at Ease

"The summit of Mount Everest is marine limestone."[1] So writes John McPhee in his book *Basin and Range*. I have no reason to doubt his knowledge. It means, of course, that at one time Mount Everest was under the sea. Talk about the faith to move mountains into the sea. Give nature time, which nature has plenty of—rocks can wait millions of years—and nature will cover the mountains with seawater.

We need the earth to survive; the earth doesn't need us. Indeed, nuclear weapons and waste put the earth at risk. I live on a ridge of the Appalachian mountains in Pennsylvania. Some 3.6 billion years ago this earth was thrust up, by virtue of continental collision down by the Piedmont. "The endless mountain," as the Lenape Indians called it, buckled up, forming a ridge. The ridge, the wild life, the plant life, and the rocks got on very well for those billions of years until humankind appeared on the scene.

Humanoid creatures emerged some five to eight million years ago, according to current theories of paleontology and anthropology. There is some evidence that humans, gorillas, and orangutans came from a common ancestor. So we are kissin' cousins, in fact, if we go back far enough. But now we are threatening not only our cousins of all kinds, but the precious ozone layer around our atmosphere, our sky, which is, as Lewis Thomas writes, "The World's Biggest Membrane."

When the earth came alive it began constructing its own membrane, for the general purpose of editing the sun. . . . Now we are protected against lethal ultraviolet rays by a narrow rim of ozone, thirty miles out. We are safe, well ventilated, and incubated, provided we can avoid technologies that might fiddle with that ozone, or shift the levels of carbon dioxide. Oxygen is not a major worry for us, unless we let fly with enough nuclear explosives to kill off the green cells in the sea; if we do that, of course, we are in for strangling . . . Taken all in all, the sky is a miraculous achievement. It works, and for what it is designed to accomplish, it is as infallible as anything in nature. I doubt whether any of us could think of a way to improve on it, beyond maybe shifting a local cloud from here to there on occasion. The word "chance" does not serve to account well for structures of such magnificence. There may have been elements of luck in the emergence of chloroplasts, but once these things were on the scene, the evolution of the sky became absolutely ordained. Chance suggests alternatives, other possibilities, different solutions. This may be true for gills, and swim-bladders, and forebrains, matters of detail, but not for the sky. There is simply no other way to go. We should credit it for what it is: for sheer size and perfection of function, it is far and away the grandest product of collaboration in all of nature. It breathes for us, and it does another thing for our pleasure. Each day, millions of meteorites fall against the outer limits of the membrane and are burned to nothing by the friction. Without this shelter, our surface would long since have become the pounded powder of the moon. Even though our receptors are not sensitive enough to hear it, there is comfort in knowing that the sound is there overhead, like the random noise of rain on the roof at night.[2]

The earth comforts and shelters us. We don't comfort and shelter the earth but more often extract its riches, leaving it scarred and vulnerable. We forget that the earth is not our creature. We are creatures of the earth. The earth does not need us to survive. We need the earth to survive. So we blink and grope towards a seachange of consciousness (another skinning of the eyes) where we understand and experience ourselves to be like the fetus with its placenta. We are the fetus; the earth and atmosphere function as our placenta.

We depend on the natural environment for survival, as a fetus depends on its mother's womb. Except that we have for a long time been imagining it the other way around. In her book *Patriarchy as a Conceptual Trap*, Elizabeth Dodson Gray graphs out a pyramid-shaped picture of the way we have viewed things in a patriarchal culture.[3] At the top of the pyramid is God; underneath God are men; then women, children, animals, plants—nature—in that descending order. We *rank* diversity rather than marvel at it and enjoy it. In this hierarchical paradigm, the idea has been that the lower orders serve and adapt to the higher ones. So, plants and animals service humanity, children obey parents, women serve and obey men, and so on up to God.

Dodson Gray calls this picture an "anthropocentric illusion." We have confused "uniqueness with superiority," and our version of stewardship is a paternalism, sometimes benign, often malign . . . as at Love Canal, or

Times Beach, Missouri, or whenever/wherever we exploit nature's resources without regard for replenishment or restoration. (The fact is that we humans don't know enough yet to know what's best for nature. We just don't know what 24,000 years of radiation from plutonium stored by us in the rocks somewhere will do to the earth. There is growing awareness now that all-out nuclear war might destroy the ozone layer, resulting in what Jonathan Schell calls "a republic of insects and grass.")[4] But we are living with a faulty paradigm of the ways things really are—an upside down one, in fact. In order for the healing of history to happen, there will have to be a healing of creation.

I am writing this now in April. If April is the cruelest month, then May in Pennsylvania may be the kindest one. May is the month when orange-black orioles, indigo buntings, and rose-breasted grosbeaks stop by our forest and feeders on their northward journey. We look in our bird log (we don't have a people log) and note that the grosbeaks are two weeks ahead of last year's time table, and the bunting is on schedule to the day. We put out the sunflower seeds and watch our visitors' dipping/swooping choreography. We take comfort in the turning of the seasons and the burgeoning truth that "the whole creation is . . . groaning in one great act of giving birth." And we're part of it, for "we too groan inwardly as we wait for our bodies to be set free" (Rom. 8:20-23 JB).

For biblical people there is no dichotomy between the God of history and the God of nature. There is one God over all, in all, and through all. We hear our own groaning with their voices in the fluted notes of the wood thrush, the gurgling mountain brook, and the random noise of rain on the roof!

Hans Küng speaks of the kingdom of God as "God's creation healed." I like that, and I like it even better as "God's creation healing"—acknowledging the process of God's creative power even now healing earth, history, the nations, us. Sometimes I can't believe it. But the return of the orioles and their friends helps.

Humor and humility both derive from the same root—humus, earth. To be in touch with the earth, as our Native American sisters and brothers have long understood, is to have our souls cleansed of human chauvinism. To be earthy is to enjoy the habits, and respect the habitats, of our creaturely friends. To be grounded is to slip into a banana peel perspective, allowing us to laugh at our beautiful ungainly bodies and to entertain a self-mockery that helps keep us humane. Laughless people are the most dangerous.

Matthew Fox reminds us that it is time to reappropriate a theology of pleasure. He suggests there are three dimensions to eating bread and drinking wine. First, to eat the substance itself and drink the fluid—savoring the pleasure of tasting, swallowing, taking nourishment. Second is to eat and drink the elements as a gift—experiencing an overflowing thankfulness, sensing that life itself is gift, and knowing the joy of renewing and refreshing our bodies. Third is to know that we eat and drink that which is eternally not other—it is itself and has its own integrity of being.

Pleasure is a profound political issue. People are changed by pleasure. There is a connection between repression of pleasure and oppression of others. The West needs a theology of pleasure. Consumerism shows that we don't know how to enjoy ourselves. The realm of God is the delight in eating one piece of popcorn—slowly—savoring the salty butter crackle in our mouths. We may talk of lovers "pleasuring" one another. The psalmist sings, "In thy right hand are pleasures forevermore" (Ps. 16:11). We may experience God in the creation as delicious and voluptuous. Earth is "the erotic connection."[5]

Fox invites us to a radical trust in creation. "If you're forty, meditate on forty-one years ago. You can trust nothingness, because that's where you came from. The void can be trusted." He playfully calls this a "belly button theology."[6]

We have all received life. Before we can understand or take up our vocation of caring for creation, we need to acknowledge that we are being cared for by creation and have been cared for since the moment of our conception. We need to be able to let ourselves go and let ourselves be . . . in grace, to know that breathing is a gift, given moment by moment. For me, following Meister Eckhart, the image of "sinking" is gracious.

One of the reasons that swimming is a primary way for me to allow my body to mingle with creation is that I can sink into the water without much fear. I learned to swim when very young, and therefore have not been afraid to dive into or fall into deeper water, knowing that I would rise to the surface. Swimming is one way I can easily let go control of my body, my life, my history—experience the buoyancy and support of the water, and rediscover that there is a flowing, easy place for me to live and move and have my being. It is a diving into "the divine soup," as Fox puts it.

The symbol of the early church was a fish under

water. The symbol of the church of Peter, or what has become the institutional church, is a bark above water. Peter's church has become too dry—it is beached, no participative enough but is too much on top of things, reflecting the patriarchal trap of which Dodson Gray writes. Our theology issues from the top down instead of the ground up, including that of Tillich, whose "ground of being" was still largely conceptual and rational. When Eckhart prays, "I pray God to rid me of God," he was praying for the particular screens and scales of his own cultural mindset to be removed so that the light of God could shine clear in and through him.[7] When we pray, "I pray God to rid me of God," we might be praying for God to rid of us the male God, the Western God, the American God, the Methodist God—whatever partial screens filter out, instead of in, the God who is God, the I-Am-That-I-Am, the I-Will-Be-Who-I-Will-Be.

Our survival as human beings in this nuclear age depends in part upon our allowing ourselves to be nourished by the earth—to enjoy, savor, and delight in the earth and its pleasures and beauty and pain. We are in need of allowing ourselves to join the entire creation now in our toxic and psychic poisoning—groaning and yearning to be healed.

> I can hear, underground, that sucking and sobbing,
> In my veins, in my bones I feel it,—
> The small waters seeping upward,
> The tight grains parting at last.
> When sprouts break out,
> Slippery as fish,
> I quail, lean to beginnings, sheath-wet.[8]

Our Native American sisters and brothers understood that there is no healing of history save as there is a healing of earth and of our bodies. The healing of body and soul, of nature and history, is interconnected and dialectical. "With all beings and all things we are as relatives." Such earthy theology yields worship that is curved, gathering around a circle, a medicine wheel of creation. We need "a whole-system ethic."[9] If something is not good for *any* part of the system, it is not good for *my* part of the system. We live in an interconnected ecosystem. We can never only do one thing. DDT is in the tissues even of penguins in the Antarctic. There is no "away" to throw things to, as we are learning with regard to nuclear wastes. If something is not good for women, it is not good for men either. If it's not good for Russians, it's not good for Americans. The attempt at political or economic strangulation of another nation simply endangers our own. If something is not good for the earth, it is not good for humans. Russell Baker suggests that if "ring around the collar" is unfortunate for the individual, "ring around the river" is unfortunate for the whole community![10]

"Love your enemies" is an ethical imperative affirming a whole system. It is in our *self-interest* to love our enemies. Loving our enemies does not mean yielding our interests to theirs, but recognizing that our deepest and longest interests are mutual. Ecologically, Dodson Gray suggests that we design our human enterprises as hands into gloves that are already there. We must do our "ecological reconnaisance," and evolve technology that is responsive to and respectful of natural systems. Our technology can become more sensuous. There is an erotic connection with the environment waiting to be touched and embraced.

A few years ago, architects and engineers developed a highway along and around Grandfather Mountain in North Carolina. The path of the highway followed the curving ridge of the mountain. The stone of the highway walls bore the same colors as the rock of the mountain. The highway excited the interest and care of the workers so that it became a thing of joy to work on and help create—a modest Chartres of roadbuilding, where the earth and its materials found respect and yielded appropriate beauty of function and appearance. Mountains have been raped. This time they were made love to.

The earth and its resources are not here to serve humanity nor is humanity here to serve the earth, but we are all here to care for and be cared for. There is a mutual care and nourishment going on. The birds and I nourish one another. There is an exchange that leaves each of us the healthier, and certainly me happier.

Stewardship is in process of redefinition. Jeremy Rifkin and Ted Howard in *The Emerging Order: God in the Age of Scarcity* note that God's first commandment, "Have dominion over the birds of the air and the fish of the sea . . ." is now being redefined. Christian theology for centuries has used the old concept of dominion "to justify unrestrained pillage and exploitation of the natural world. . . . The new concept is that dominion is stewardship rather than ownership and conservation rather than exploitation. This belief is at loggerheads with . . . the Reformation . . . world view. . . . The Calvinist individual who . . . sought salvation through productivity and the exploitation of nature is now being challenged by a Christian person who seeks salvation

by conserving and protecting God's creation."[11] Rifkin
and Howard suggest that the earlier Protestant work
ethic is being replaced by a conservation ethic. Or we
could say that a rebalancing is taking place, a search for
harmony, a mutuality of work and play.

The first covenant God made was nonverbal, and it
was to the earth.[12] God made the earth, gave life to the
earth, invested energy in it, committed vitality to it. The
covenant with creation was a total risk of self-giving on
God's part. God set the rainbow in the clouds as a sign of
the covenant, and as a pledge that God would not allow
a flood to destroy the earth again. Seven times in these
brief Genesis verses a reference appears to the covenant
of God wth "every living creature." The covenant
begins with Noah and his descendants, but immediately
includes every living creature. It is a covenant "between
me and the earth" (Gen. 9:7-17).

That is a creation-centered theology. The earth has
value to God with or without human beings. Value is
creation-based.[13] In that foundational sense, "Whatever
is, is right" (Pope). Whatever is, is holy. Robert Louis
Stevenson prayed, "Lord, thou sendest down rain upon
the uncounted millions of the forest, and givest the
trees to drink exceedingly. We are here upon this isle a
few handfuls of men, and how many myriads upon
myriads of stalwart trees! Teach us the lesson of the
trees. The sea around us, which this rain recruits, teems
with the race of fish; teach us, Lord, the meaning of the
fishes. Let us see ourselves for what we are, one of the
countless number of the clans of thy handiwork. When
we would despair, let us remember that these also
please and serve Thee."[14]

The meaning of the fishes! My wife has let me into

her communion with whales. On both coasts, off Mendocino in northern California and Provincetown in Massachusetts, we have gone to watch the whales—those gentle giants, breeching before us—as it seemed, for us—playing, sporting. One day on the bluff over Mendocino, we saw forty-three gray whales spouting their way south to the tip of Baja on their eight thousand mile round-trip underwater from Alaska . . . down to breed and calve—those large-brained creatures who communicate to each other (picked up by sonar). I have read that sometimes one male whale will serve as a couch for another male and female to make love. Magnanimity, that!

> And bull-whales gather their women and whale-calves in a ring
> when danger threatens, on the surface of the ceaseless flood
> and range themselves like great fierce Seraphim facing the threat
> encircling their huddled monsters of love.
> and all this happiness in the sea, in the salt
> where God is also love, but without words . . .[15]

When we seek to protect the whales, we seek to protect part of our own history swimming before our eyes—brother sun, sister moon, cousin whale. The bull was the animal of imagination for the Greeks, the buffalo for the American Indian. When we killed the buffalo, we killed something in the soul of the American Indian. "O give me a home where the buffalo roam" is now a lament. The buffalo are gone. How am I diminished because the buffalo are gone? How would we be diminished if the whales were gone? What does another species mean to the healing of our soul, the healing of our human nature? The healing of creation? Somehow there is a connection, an interconnection. We can never only do one thing. When one species is lost, we are diminished. Henry Beston puts it this way:

> We need another and a wiser and perhaps a more mystical concept of animals. Remote from universal nature, and living by complicated artifice, man in civilization surveys the creature through the glass of his knowledge and sees thereby a feather magnified and the whole image in distortion. We patronize them for their incompleteness, for their tragic fate of having taken form so far below ourselves. And therein we err, and greatly err. For the animal shall not be measured by man. In a world older and more complete than ours they move finished and complete, gifted with extensions of the senses we have lost or never attained, living by voices we shall never hear. They are not brethren; they are not underlings; they are other nations, caught with ourselves in the net of life and time, fellow prisoners of the splendor and travail of the earth.[16]

We are one of the clans, one of the tribes, one of the nations of creatures on the earth. We are the clan with moral responsibility to care for, appreciate, enjoy, savor, and nourish the other clans. Humans are called to be caretakers of the earth, which is a better thing than to be stewards. The word *stewardship* carries a certain inevitable every member canvass taint to it or brings up images of dinner on board ship. There is a cold, abstract, monetary cant about it; the word seems drained of joy or warmth. One might be an efficient steward without caring either for the master or for the master's property. But a caretaker, by definition, takes care *of* because of caring *for*. Caretakers are in the business of helping to heal creation. Caretakers are agriculturalists of the future, seeding and watering today for the health and hope of tomorrow. The Age of Aquarius comes in as a gardener. In one of the Easter stories, Mary mistakes Jesus for the gardener (John 20:15). Blessed are the caretakers, for they shall be called the gardeners of God.

Harriet and Howell Heaney are old friends who live on Mount Airy Avenue in the Germantown section of Philadelphia. They are also blessed caretakers and gardeners. "In the November/December, 1981 issue of *The Green Scene* you can find a 5-page article . . . entitled, 'The Collector's Garden: Built from Trash and Found Objects.' The author is our own Harriet Heaney. In it she reveals how a combination of expertise, ingenuity, perseverance and TLC have transformed their one-fifth acre city plot into an amazingly abundant . . . garden. By cultivating every square inch intensively, Harriet (with Howell's assistance) keeps the household bountifully supplied with at least 20 kinds of vegetables, 20 herbs, fruit from 12 dwarf trees, currants, raspberries, blueberries, strawberries, grapes, and a variety of flowers."[17] The Heaneys use such imaginative devices as rotating the soil, not the plants, transplanting to build up strength and conserve space, creating organic fertilizers. They have learned how to orchestrate a horticultural symphony. Blessed are the caretakers, for they shall be called the gardeners of God.

Theodore Roethke grew up near a greenhouse,

where his father and those who helped him were
growers of plants and flowers. One of his poems reads:

> Gone the three ancient ladies
> Who creaked on the greenhouse ladders,
> Reaching up white strings
> To wind, to wind
> The sweet-pea tendrils . . .
> They tied and tucked,—
> These nurses of nobody else.
> Quicker than birds, they dipped
> Up and sifted the dirt;
> They sprinkled and shook; . . .
> Like witches they flew along rows
> Keeping creation at ease;
> With a tendril for needle
> They sewed up the air with a stem;
> They teased out the seed that the cold
> > kept asleep,—
> All the coils, loops, and whorls.
> They trellised the sun; they plotted
> > for more than themselves.[18]

Three gardeners for God, plotting for more than
themselves, giving the gift of tomorrow, keeping
creation at ease.

The Cornucopia Project is an organization of people
plotting for more than themselves. They are working
for a constructive transformation of the U.S. food
system, citing such frightening facts as that 4.8 billion
tons of soil are eroded from the nation's agricultural
areas each year, and that for every $1.00 we spend to
grow food, we spend another $1.00 moving it around
(cross-country shipping). The project's aims include:

1. A degree of regionalization of the U.S. food system.
2. The substitution of renewable resources for non-renew-

able resources and an increase in efficiency of resource utilization in all aspects of the food system.

3. The increased protection of the environmental support system vital to the food system.

4. A renewed emphasis on locally available fresh food.

5. The increased availability of participation by those members of the food system who want to be actively involved in the decision-making for the food system.

6. An increase in the agricultural productivity and economic democracy through the renewed emphasis on smaller and more intensive food production systems.[19]

Yet another measure would be to institute local and regional marketing co-ops or to encourage existing supermarkets or farmers' markets that would buy from any scale of regional food producer—from backyard gardener, to truck farmer, to large regional farmer, thereby providing a market for any food surplus. An early 1983 newsletter from the Cornucopia Project reports that "an alternative food network in Hartford, Connecticut, has already established five farmers' markets, 22 community gardens, four food buying clubs, two solar greenhouses, and a community 'self-help' cannery. During the last decade more than 4,000 food buying clubs and co-ops have begun eliminating the work done by costly distributors and retailers, at a savings by as much as 30 percent to consumers."[20]

Unfortunately, those in charge of preserving and protecting our nation's resources have *not* plotted for more than themselves and have been destroying the gift of tomorrow while diseasing creation. Former Interior Secretary James Watt was "selling off up to 35 million acres of public lands . . . vastly accelerating the amount of Federal coal properties leased or sold . . . [planning to] double the amount of timber cut from national forests by the year 2000, [trying] to open several of our last remaining wilderness areas to oil and gas drilling . . . striving to lease virtually all the remaining one billion acres of coastal waters to oil companies . . . This economic folly is compounded by Mr. Watt's arrogance: 'I have never been criticized by anyone I respect.' His missionary zeal to immediately liquidate Federal assets, denies our heirs any voice in determining whether, when and how their trust principal might be sold."[21] Watt has said that he intended to "cannibalize" the National Park Service by transferring its officials elsewhere. What irony that a supposed conservative administration should so recklessly *fail* to conserve, protect, cherish, and preserve the national treasure of our natural heritage.

Caretakers of creation are responsible for earth-care.

In August 1982 I spent several days in a poetry and prose workshop led by poet Robert Bly. Every morning we met under a tree down by the lake and were instructed to go pick up a rock, flower, stick, piece of fern, dragonfly, piece of bark, whatever. Our task then was to spend several minutes examining the specimen, observing its size, colors, weight, shape, smell, taste, sounds, texture. Bly said that poetry consists of introspection and observation. We were getting lessons in observation, and I learned quickly that I had majored in introspection and knew little of observation. Indeed, beyond observation of pieces of earth, I have not observed people well in my life. So intent have I been on promoting my own ideas, agendas, plans, and projecting them on other people and situations, that I have not been patient, still enough inside, humble enough before other realities . . . just to observe what was there.

"Do you see this woman?" (Luke 7:44) asked Jesus of Simon. No, Simon had not seen the woman; he already knew what kind of woman she was. Bob, do you see this fragile Queen Anne's lace?

> One wading a Fall meadow finds on all sides
> The Queen Anne's Lace lying like lilies
> On water; it glides
> So from the walker, it turns
> Dry grass to a lake, as the slightest shade of you
> Valleys my mind in fabulous blue Lucernes.[22]

We repeated the poem over and over until it became like a gentle Bach fugue curling around again and again. There was a gentle rhythm—the wading and gliding and turning and valleying rolled through all things . . . so that the following September, I *saw* the Queen Anne's lace by the farmhouse along the road . . . as though I had never seen it before.

I am slowly learning to observe "the lovely diminutives" (Roethke) of creation. And what affectionate looks go back and forth. I have long noticed the birds. I say long—for perhaps twelve years. One time I jotted down the movements I had seen, thinking of all the many-splendored verbs describing the birds' glorious flight . . . veering, dipping, diving, flying, racing, pitching, skipping, hopping, twittering, bending, leaping, springing, quivering, flinging, scuttling, pecking, knocking, blowing, swooping, careening . . . such fun! I must confess that I have not always kept my patience with the squirrels that sometimes invade our feeders, especially the red ones.

I am learning that a dead tree in the backyard is not only potential firewood, but also the favorite pecking place of a masterly flicker. If I want the flicker as a neighbor, I may have to leave that dead tree standing there. I may have to choose between flickers and firewood.

Neighbors decided to drain the swamp in their backyard a few years ago. And they have nurtured the swamp to become a less mosquito-infested burgeoning garden. But the wood ducks that used to nest there in the marshy close are gone.

Years ago my daughters kept after me to stop shampooing my hair in the lake—Glen Lake. I had been washing my hair there for over thirty years, and loved the feel of getting my hair all soapy and then diving in and swimming twenty or thirty feet underwater, coming up with hair clear of soap. They persuaded me that even though the pollution from power boats in the lake was worse than an occasional glob of shampoo in the water, I had to stop doing it for my own integrity. So I did. It wasn't much to give up so as to plot for more than myself. And blessed joy, a couple of years later, my son came across a shampoo that was natural, biodegradable, and OK to use in the lake!

The entire creation is groaning, singing, slurping, slithering, sobbing, oozing with . . . life! But we are pushing it toward death. We know about the more than four hundred Superfund sites in this country where there is major toxic hazard to the health of people and earth. We have to keep asking ourselves what is nourishing to the earth and what is toxic. Love Canal is a three-blocks long dump where Hooker Chemical poured over 20,000 tons of chemical waste from

1947-1952. Times Beach, Missouri, is a town where dioxin was laid down in road cover, back ten to twelve years ago. The EPA estimates that fifty-seven million tons of chemical waste are annually dumped here and there around our neighborhoods. Creation's groans are now become consonant with our own. There is an earth wisdom. If we pollute the earth, it will eventually pollute us because we cannot escape the earth—we belong here. Some Mormons and others in Utah discovered that God did not want their holy land to become a network of missile tracks and silos. Other folks have discovered that all land is holy, and God doesn't want *any* of it to become a doomsday launch or sponge. The sea and the air are God's, too. Holy space all.

There is an interweaving of place and people, of person and environment. Love Canal is a cancer in the body of the earth. The nuclear submarine originally namd *Corpus Christi* smells with the same rot. Drought discloses that those down the river can have enough, only if we conserve water where we live. Infection—and healing—spread.

There was a dump out beside the farmhouse road near Kirkridge. It had been there for years. People would drive down the farmhouse road, or come secretly in their jeeps and pickups up the powerline cutting and drop off broken lamps, mattresses, stoves, tires, springs, bureaus. The dump was on somebody else's land.

For years anger built in us while nothing was done to heal the festering dump-sore. We preferred to live in self-righteous anger at our neighbor's indifference, rather than take initiative ourselves. It was too big a task. It would cost too much, and so on. Until one day we decided to clean it up . . . and found that it took less time and money to do it than we had supposed. We removed the largest objects, pushed dirt over the debris, and now . . . new green and yellow shoots cover that former excrescence. When I walk out the farmhouse road and cast a look over to my right—and see the healing of the earth—I am filled with an unreasonable joy.

Caretakers of creation are responsible for earth-care, and for body-care.

What is nourishing and what is toxic for our bodies? The first year when cigarette sales in America declined, after decades of continual growth, was 1979. There began at that time a great promotion to sell cigarettes in the Third World. Industry spokespeople said they expected the biggest profits in the 1980s to come from the Third World—where, of course, people are less well-informed about the links between smoking and cancer than in this country. The connections between profits and death: we saw it for years in Nestles' refusal to stop promoting bottle-feeding to Third World mothers, even though the evidence of its death-dealing effects on their children was clear.

What is it about us that keeps us doing deadly things to our bodies? I *won't* give up my Scotch and water before dinner. I *will* eat less meat. At that Bly workshop, which was held at the Omega Center in New York State, the food was vegetarian. I ate it, and it was delicious for five days, but I yielded to a Big Mac attack when I drove home. At Kirkridge we have eliminated junk food. We serve no red meat now, occasionally chicken or fish. Brownies hung on for quite a time. We struggle with the tension between our private eating habits and what we serve to our retreatants by way of seeking to embody our espoused values. What goes into our mouths is as important as what comes out of our mouths.

In Canada there is a law about wearing seat belts in the car, and if the police see you not wearing your seat belt, you are fined $28. Statistics all over the world demonstrate that wearing a seat belt is much safer than not wearing one. A New York state billboard shows a picture of a state trooper, saying, "I have never yet unbelted a dead person." Yet, less than 15 percent of Americans use seat belts. What is that about? Some confusion of personal freedom with personal safety? Or some dangerous laziness? What is it that keeps us from simply taking care of our bodies?

Exercise is in, of course. Diet books and exercise books lead the best seller lists. I brought home a headline from the *National Enquirer* one time, and we put it up on the refrigerator. It read: "The Ecstasy Diet: Eat all you like in 1983, yet . . . LOSE 25-30 lbs. BY MAKING LOVE."[23] I didn't read the article. I just liked the idea. If there's a Pritikin diet and a Scarsdale diet, why not an ecstasy diet?

Body care. Body wisdom. It comforts me to walk on the earth, not on the sidewalk or the street, but the earth. It nourishes me to climb over rocks, not staircases. The exercise may be the same, but the soul healing is not. Making love is healing. Sometimes for a moment, we may see and be seen, and know "who touched me" (Mark 5:31). The body reveals the soul as well as conceals it.

Caretakers of creation are responsible for building care—
the care of houses, streets, cities, subways. Restoration work began in 1967 of York Minster in

England, the seat of the Archbishop of York. The cathedral had been eaten through by the death-watch beetle. When restoration was completed, there was not only a sound foundation for the cathedral but also an organ sonata. Curious workmen had asked the organist what note their drills made as they cut into the stone for the installation of steel rods to strengthen the foundation. The organist said, "E-flat," and when the work was over, he played a sonata he had composed—

The Rebirth of a Cathedral in E-flat.

The last few years we have been restoring our 1815 farmhouse at Kirkridge. We've been composing with nail and hammer, ringing out a plain song in A-sharp! The hearth-stones of the farmhouse were set up in 1815. For more than one hundred and twenty-five years, farm families cooked their food, read their books, and warmed their bodies at that hearth. In the last forty years, thousands of people have made pilgrimage to sit before those stones, listening for their silent stories, telling their own. What stories are frozen in these stones: stories of confessions heard, wounds healed, songs shared, friendship sealed? Is this a house of God? Surely the Lord is in this place! (Gen. 28:10-22).

There are houses, buildings, and stones that mark holy space for each of us—places where God has become manifest to us in such manner that we were amazed by grace, knew the Presence, and wanted to mark the memory. René Dubos wrote that when the words *genius* or *spirit* are used to denote the distinctive characteristics of a given region, city, institution, or place, there is implied . . . "the tacit acknowledgment that each place possesses a set of attributes that determine the uniqueness of its landscape and its people."[24] San Francisco and Boston, for example, despite the changes in each city over the centuries, retain their own unique genius, spirit, flavor—that enduring ambience of tangible character that is both given and made. Dubos is speaking for the significance of place, places where pillows become pillars, bushes begin burning, and earth is filled with treasure—stones with stories to tell. The Kirkridge farmhouse was built on a hillside of the Appalachian ridge, those ancient rocks thrust up some 3.6 billion years ago. Once the Lenape Indians roamed, hunted, and fished here. That Native American dignity abides on the mountainside, though wounded by more recent excavations, buildings, and tree cutting. I have heard it said that we are hacking out a view. And these hills whence cometh our help do show signs of having been hacked.

Still, these farmhouse stones glow with stories. These dining tables become Emmaus tables where hearts and eyes are opened, and we know the Lord has surely been among us. Carved into the wooden mantelpiece of another Pennsylvania farmhouse, this one built in 1750 and now an inn, are words of the poet Horace: *"Ille Terrarum Mihi Prater Omnes Angulus Ridet"*—"This corner of the earth smiles on me above all others."

In the silent dark around the hearth, I marvel at these old rafter beams and all they have heard, seen, welcomed, and witnessed. A cloud of witnesses indeed! The spirits of those gone before us now abide in the mystery of beam and stone. A comfort to know we do not make our journey alone but are surrounded and supported by all the saints. A cloud of witnesses above and below. Gioia Timpanelli writes, "The dead are holding hands under the earth."[25] Under the earth. We are standing on their shoulders. We depend on them and they support us. It is the custom of the Moravians in Bethlehem, Pennsylvania, to gather on Easter morning in the great graveyard by the Mother Church and sing praises to the risen Christ, standing on the gravestones of their ancestors.

The modesty of this farmhouse—it is comfortable here, not threatening. One can let the roles and masks slip off in the dark, without being noticed or noticing. It seems a safe and blessed place. "In every place where I cause my name to be remembered, I will come to you and bless you." Lord, come to us and bless us. There are angels here, but demons too. This is a place to let the demons out and wrestle them to a painful blessing, a place to acknowledge wounds and become wounded healers. In the sharing is the healing. Pilgrim souls are restored as strangers find welcome. This is a place of ease and gentle care. A place for taking care. Surely the Lord is in this place. How awesome is this place!

The rebirth of a cathedral in E-flat, the renovation of a farmhouse in A-sharp! Some years ago Paul Winter invited twenty friends to spend the summer at his farm, creating a living village of drummers, singers, instrumentalists, cooks, healers, poets, and neighbors. It became a forum of fertile intermingling of life streams and stories, myths and folklore. Winter and his musician friends made records, juxtaposing sounds from the wild—whales, a timber wolf, and an eagle . . . with the sounds of saxaphone, clarinet, flute—a consort, a harmony of creatures wild and human. "Sometime after having gathered these creature songs, I found to my amazement that all three were in the key of D-flat. I've enjoyed speculating on whether this is a lucky coincidence, or a gift from the Muse. I was told by a teacher once that in some esoteric systems, D-flat is considered to be the key of the earth."[26]

Does all creation groan in this key? Robert Bly notes that the degree of curve of a centuries-old mosque in Iran and that of a snail shell oceans away are identical—.0618. Is there a spiral curve of the universe? There is surely a patterning, a curving possibility, a yearning towards some sort of unity. Some cosmologists today are seeking to *quanticize gravity*. That means finding a fully qualified law of gravity and quantum mechanics, seeking to solve the "quantum-gravity problem, bringing gravity in under the quantum tent with the rest of physics, and thereby producing (or at least inducing) a great theory that explains the behavior of all matter," seeking insights about unifying laws and about the beginning and end of the universe.[27]

I don't understand it, of course, but I believe in it and towards it!

There is a yearning for wholeness, for coming round home again, for the circle of the universe. The Native American understood this in the use of the medicine wheel, which contained all the earth, all forms of life within the wheel; each direction had a special color and animal. Each tepee opened with a hole at the top where the pole of the universe came in, to root in the center of the universe. Everything in the universal wheel knows of harmony except humankind. We have to reach out to the four corners of the universe and travel to other parts to integrate wholeness. Isaiah sang out of a similar vision: "I will bring your offspring from the east, and from the west I will gather you; I will say to the north,

Give up, and to the south, Do not withhold; bring my sons from afar and my daughters from the end of the earth, every one who is called by my name" (Isa. 43:5b-7).

Jesus' image of the kingdom of God's creation healing was a homecoming banquet where all the children of the earth, including the least of our sisters and brothers and even you and me, will sit at table in the mother-father's house. Home as family circle, a circle that erupted at Pentecost to include people of every nation on earth. That biblical vision includes the presence of angels and beasts, as at the birth of Jesus, in a peaceable kingdom where the entire creation groaning for redemption will find it together . . . where the lion and lamb shall lie down together, and we shall not destroy in all the Lord's holy mountain.

We caretakers of creation, by skinning our eyes, doing our hope-work, facing our enemies, and keeping creation at ease, seek the grace and peace of God where we can find it.

> When despair for the world grows in me
> and I wake in the night at the least sound
> in fear of what my life and my children's lives may be,
> I go and lie down where the wood drake
> rests in his beauty on the water, and the great heron feeds.
> I come into the peace of wild things
> who do not tax their lives with forethought
> of grief. I come into the presence of still water.
> And I feel above me the day-blind stars
> waiting with their light. For a time
> I rest in the grace of the world, and am free.[28]

Notes

1. Sweeping Up the Heart

1. James Agee, *A Death in the Family* (New York: Grosset & Dunlap, 1957), pp. 82-83.

2. Poem written by author after reflection upon father's death.

3. Emily Dickinson, "The Bustle in a House," in *The Complete Poems of Emily Dickinson*, Thomas H. Johnson, ed. (Boston: Little, Brown & Co., 1960), p. 489.

4. Robert Raines, *Going Home* (San Francisco: Harper & Row, 1979), p. 33.

5. Henri J. M. Nouwen, *The Living Reminder* (New York: Seabury Press, 1977), p. 44.

6. Frederick Buechner, *The Sacred Journey* (San Francisco: Harper & Row, 1982), p. 74.

7. George Herold, lay lecturer of First United Methodist Church of Germantown in Philadelphia, Pa., used this phrase about his church.

8. Robert Bly, "The Prodigal Son," in *The Man in the Black Coat Turns* (New York: Dial Press, 1981), p. 7.

9. Dietrich Bonhoeffer, *Letters and Papers from Prison,* enlarged ed., ed. Eberhard Bethge (New York: Macmillan Publishing Co., 1971), p. 87.

2. The Turning Circle

1. Jonathan Schell, *The Fate of the Earth* (New York: Alfred A. Knopf, 1982), p. 144.

2. Schell, pp. 174-75.

3. Herbert Tarr, *The Conversion of Chaplain Cohen* (New York: Bernard Geis Associates, 1963).

4. Mary Bateson, "Caring for Children, Caring for the Earth," *Christianity and Crisis*, 40, No. 5, 31 Mar. 1980, p. 69.

5. Erik Erikson, *Identity and the Life Cycle* (New York: W. W. Norton, 1980), p. 103.

6. Erik Erikson, *Insight and Responsibility* (New York: W. W. Norton, 1964), pp. 130-31.

7. Marie-Louise von Franz, *Projection and Re-collection in Jungian Psychology* (London: Open Court Press, 1980), pp. 30-31.

8. Carl G. Jung, *The Portable Jung,* ed. Joseph Campbell (New York: Penguin Books, 1971), pp. 17-18.

9. Walker Percy, *The Second Coming* (New York: Farrar, Straus & Giroux, 1980), p. 125.

10. Morris West, *The Clowns of God* (New York: William Morrow & Co., 1981), p. 42.

11. William Stringfellow, *A Simplicity of Faith* (Nashville: Abingdon Press, 1982), p. 21.

3. By the Skin of Our Eyes

1. Schell, p. 118.

2. Wallace Turner, "Cabinet Officer Says U.S. Will Continue Atom Arms Testing," *New York Times,* 6 Aug. 1982, Sec. B, p. 4, col. 6.

3. *Ridgeleaf,* Kirkridge newsletter, Dec. 1982.

4. Jim Wallis, "Marginal Notes," *Sojourners,* Feb. 1983, p. 25.

5. Peggy Scherer, "Peace, A Gift From God," *The Catholic Worker,* Dec. 1982, p. 2.

4. Hope-Work

1. Thomas Keneally, *Schindler's List* (New York: Simon & Schuster, 1982), pp. 322-24.

2. *The Star Ledger* [Hartford, Conn.], 25 Nov. 1982, p. 86.

3. "A Gallup Poll On Nuclear War," *Newsweek,* 5 Oct. 1981, p. 35.

4. Robert Lifton, "The Psychic Toll of the Nuclear Age," *New York Times,* 26 Sept. 1982, p. 52.

5. Joanna Macy, *Despairwork* (Philadelphia: New Society Publishers, 1982), pp. 17-18.

6. Macy, p. 26.

7. George Kennan, *The Nuclear Delusion* (New York: Pantheon Books, 1982).

8. Samuel H. Day, Jr., "The New Resistance," *The Progressive,* 23 Apr. 1982, p. 22.

9. Dorothee Soelle, "Resistance: Towards a First World Theology," *Christianity and Crisis,* 39, No. 12, 23 July 1979, p. 181.

10. Albert Camus, *Resistance, Rebellion and Death* (New York: Modern Library, 1963).

11. Robert McFadden, "Day of Protest: Many Faces, A Single Cause, A Spectrum of Humanity Represented at the Rally," *New York Times,* 13 June 1982, Sec. 1, p. 42, col. 1.

12. Keneally, p. 318.

13. Art Buchwald, "Innocent Name Hides Violence of Mega-Death Weapons," *Washington Post.*

14. Russell Baker, "Observer: The Incide Dope," *New York Times,* 1 December 1982, Sec. A, p. 31, col. 6.

15. *New York Times,* 1 Dec. 1982, Sec. C, p. 1.

16. Leonard Silk, "Cost-Effective Job Creation," *New York Times,* 22 Sept. 1982, Sec. D, p. 2, col. 3.

17. Anthony Lewis, "Abroad at Home: Hazardous to Health," *New York Times,* 28 Oct. 1982, Sec. A, p. 31, cols. 1, 2.

18. Ibid.

19. Thomas Merton, "Letter to a Young Activist," *Prophet in the Belly of a Paradox,* ed. Gerald Twomey (Chicago: Paulist Press, 1978).

20. Moshe Bejski, Supreme Court of Israel, quoted on jacket of Keneally, *Schindler's List.*

5. Facing Our Enemies

1. Raines, *Going Home,* pp. 7-12.

2. Parker Palmer, comments at Kirkridge retreat, Jan. 1983; Parker Palmer, *The Company of Strangers* (New York: Crossroad, 1981), p. 124.

3. J. W. Stevenson, *God in My Unbelief* (New York: Harper & Brothers, 1960), pp. 31-32.

4. Anthony Lewis, "Abroad at Home: Onward Christian Soldiers," *New York Times,* 10 Mar. 1983, Sec. A, p. 27, col. 1.

5. Michael Clark, presentation at Kirkridge Conference on peacemaking, Jan. 1982.

6. Schell, pp. 152-53.

7. Keith Brown, "Love and Justice Different," *Sunday Globe,* 30 Jan. 1983, Sec. A, p. 7, col. 2.

8. Schell, p. 134.

9. Hal Lindsay, *The 1980's: Countdown to Armageddon* (King of Prussia, Pennsylvania: Westgate Press, 1980), pp. 188-93.

10. George Kennan, "A Brief Against Nuclear 'Overkill,' " *Boston Globe,* 31 May 1981. The article is drawn from remarks delivered by Kennan on the 1981 occasion of his receiving the Albert Einstein Peace Prize in Washington, D.C.

11. Gordon Adams, *The Iron Triangle: The Politics of Defense Contracting* (New York: Economic Council of Priorities, 1981).

12. Robert Reinhold, "Pentagon Renews Ties with Colleges," *New York Times,* 18 May 1980, Sec. C, p. 1, col. 5.

13. Theodore H. White, "Weinberger on the Ramparts," *New York Times Magazine,* 6 Feb. 1983, Sec. 6, p. 17, col. 1.

14. Zbigniew Brzezinski, "The Failed Mission," *New York Times,* 18 Apr. 1982, Sec. 6, p. 30, col. 2.

15. Philip M. Boffey, "Social Scientists Believe Leaders Lack a Sense of War's Reality," *New York Times,* 7 Sept. 1982, Sec. C, pp. 1, 2, cols. 1, 2.

16. Boffey, Sec. C, pp. 1, 2, cols. 1, 2.

17. Steve Lohr, "11 Children of Vietnam War Head 'Home' to U.S.," *New York Times,* 1 Oct. 1982, Sec. A, p. 6, col. 5.

18. Ibid.

6. Keeping Creation at Ease

1. John McPhee, *Basin and Range* (New York: Farrar, Straus & Giroux, 1981), p. 183.

2. Lewis Thomas, *The Lives of a Cell* (New York: Viking Press, 1974), pp. 145-48.

3. Elizabeth Dodson Gray, *Patriarchy as a Conceptual Trap* (Wellesley, Mass.: Roundtable Press, 1982), p. 83.

4. Schell, p. 1.

5. Elizabeth Dodson Gray, *Green Paradise Lost* (Wellesley, Mass.: Roundtable Press, 1979), pp. 92-94.

6. Matthew Fox, presentation at a Kirkridge retreat, Mar. 1982; see also *A Spirituality Named Compassion,* and the *Healing of the Global Village, Humpty Dumpty, and Us* (Minneapolis: Winston Press, 1979).

7. Matthew Fox, *Breakthrough: Meister Eckhart's Creation Spirituality in New Translation* (New York: Doubleday, 1977), pp. 79-80.

8. Theodore Roethke, "Cuttings," in *The Collected Poems of Theodore Roethke* (New York: Doubleday/Anchor Press, 1975), p. 35.

9. Dodson Gray, *Green Paradise Lost,* pp. 76-77.

10. Russell Baker, "Observer: Ring Around the River," *New York Times,* 1982.

11. Jeremy Rifkin and Ted Howard, *The Emerging Order: God in the Age of Scarcity* (New York: Putnam Publishing Co., 1979), pp. x, 271.

12. Dodson Gray, *Green Paradise Lost,* p. 144.

13. Dodson Gray, *Green Paradise Lost,* p. 148.

14. *Robert Louis Stevenson,* "Another in Time of Rain," in *Vailima Papers* (New York: Charles Scribner's Sons); *The Prayers of Robert Louis Stevenson* (Bangor, Pa.: Kirkridge, Inc., 1982), p. 18.

15. "Whales Weep Not," in *The Complete Poems of D. H. Lawrence,* eds. Vivian De Sola Pinto and F. Warren Roberts (New York: Viking/Penguin, 1977).

16. Henry Beston, *The Outermost House* (New York: Penguin Books, 1976), p. 25.

17. Ken Connors, *Tidings,* newsletter of the First United Methodist Church of Germantown (Philadelphia, Pa.), 24, no. 7, 21 Feb. 1982.

18. Roethke, "Frau Bauman, Frau Schmidt, Frau Schwartze," in *Complete Poems,* p. 42.

19. *The Cornucopia Project: Organic Paths to Food Security* (Emmaus, Pa.: Rodale Press, 1981), p. 71.

20. Susan Kellam, *The Cornucopia Project Newsletter* (Winter 1983).

21. Thomas A. Barron, "Watt's Economic Folly," *New York Times,* 16 Feb. 1983, Sec. A, p. 31, cols. 2, 3, 4.

22. Richard Wilbur, "The Beautiful Changes," in *The Beautiful Changes and Other Poems* (New York: Reynal, 1947).

23. *National Enquirer,* 4 Jan. 1983, p. 1.

24. René Dubos, *A God Within* (New York: Charles Scribners' Sons, 1972), pp. 6-7.

25. Gioia Timpanelli, *Stones for the Hours of the Night* (New York: Rapoport Printing Co., 1978).

26. Paul Winter, Notes on the record album *Common Ground,* A & M Records, Inc., SP-4698, 1978.

27. Michael Harwood, "The Universe and Dr. Hawkins," *New York Times,* 23 Jan. 1983, Sec. 6, p. 64, col. 4.

28. Wendell Berry, "The Peace of Wild Things," in *Openings* (New York: Harcourt Brace Jovanovich, 1968).